Successes and Failures of Digital Libraries

Edited by
Susan Harum
Michael Twidale

Graduate School of Library and Information Science
University of Illinois at Urbana-Champaign
2000

© 2000 The Board of Trustees of The University of Illinois
Manufactured in the United States of America
Printed on acid-free paper
ISBN 0-87845-107-2   ISSN 0069-4789

James S. Dowling, Managing Editor
Susan Lafferty, Production Assistant
PUBLICATIONS COMMITTEE
Leigh Estabrook, Janice Del Negro, Marlo Welshons, Betsy Hearne

Contents

Give Me Documents or Give Me Death:
A Millennial Meditation on
Documents and Libraries

INTRODUCTION

The 35th Annual Clinic on Library Applications of Data Processing, entitled Successes and Failures of Digital Libraries, was organized by co-chairs Susan Harum and Michael Twidale with sponsorship from the Graduate School of Library and Information Science (GSLIS) of the University of Illinois at Urbana-Champaign (UIUC). It was held on 22-24 March 1998 at the Beckman Institute for Advanced Science and Technology on the campus of UIUC. This year's theme was deliberately provocative. Everyone enjoys discussing the successes of their project but may be rather reluctant to air the problems that arose during development. But if the development of better systems is to proceed optimally, it is just those problems that should be aired publicly.

The idea of the digital library has moved from an intriguing idea, through academic research projects, to demonstrator systems, and now arriving at real practical applications. Digital libraries already exist and many more are being planned and under construction. This clinic's goal was to address some questions that arose during the process of transition from theory and research development to deployed useful and usable (and used) systems:

- What were the problems that arose in different projects, what can we learn from them, and how can we avoid those problems in the future?
- What were the successes in projects and how can we replicate them?
- What can we learn from the work of other projects?
- How do we address the needs of end users, given limited resources?
- How should the different (and often conflicting) needs of all the stakeholders in a digital library project be reconciled?
- How should we approach the problem of integrating digital libraries with physical libraries?

- How can we achieve technology transfer from digital library research projects to practical applications?
- How can we future-proof our digital libraries in the light of constant and accelerating change in hardware, software, formats, standards, and so on?

The four-year NSF/ARPA/NASA-funded Digital Libraries Initiative (DLI) based at UIUC was entering its final year. Thus it was a good time to re-examine the development process. The idea was to use the DLI as a detailed case study from which to derive the questions outlined above in order to serve as a resource for future digital library activities. The focus on the DLI was complemented by external invited speakers giving a wider perspective. We were trying to provide valuable insights for those wanting to develop their own digital libraries.

As well as issues that might be typified as theoretical, technological and managerial aspects of digital library research, design, development, and implementation, some are aspects imparting "trade craft." In any newly emerging field, the early developers must do much tinkering in order to pursue their larger theoretical goals. In this way the trade craft of the discipline emerges. These can be rules of thumb, hints, or tricks that improve the development, implementation, or acceptance process. These are the result of considerable trial and effort but individually are often not considered profound enough to merit mention in the published research results. Thus newcomers to the field wishing to replicate or build on the efforts of the early pioneers have to reinvent this trade craft—an unnecessary and wasteful process.

As well as presentations, demonstrations of various parts of the UIUC project were made on the second evening, and the clinic was concluded with a chaired general discussion of issues and lessons learned from the DLI and other projects.

The keynote address was by Stephen Griffin, program director, Digital Libraries Initiative, National Science Foundation (NSF). He summarized the history of the Digital Library Initiative (DLI–Phase 1) and the lessons learned for the second phase including the need for wider access and development in a larger framework which included content, use, and usability of distributed knowledge generally, as well as more interaction between technologists and librarians and a wider international perspective.

Ed Fox reported on the Networked Digital Library of Theses and Dissertations. He described the ingenious mechanisms the project provides for addressing the concerns of access relating to copyright, patent processes, and prior publication regulations as thesis results are used as the basis for publication in journals. This is an example of the broader managerial/social/economic issues that have to be addressed if a digital library is to be accepted even if all the technical problems have been resolved.

Two presentations by Bruce Schatz and Bill Mischo, co-principal investigators of the DLI, surveyed the project and the broad lessons learned. The sheer size of the DLI compared to other earlier projects raises issues of scale that future digital libraries will need to consider, including all the complexities of multiple formats that arise in a heterogeneous collection from many different sources.

The next sequence of presentations considered different aspects of the DLI in depth and the particular lessons learned from that perspective. Ann Bishop and Laura Neumann reported on studies of the usability of the DLI and the importance of considering the wider context of the use of information resources. They noted the problem of a large number of users "bailing out" of the system and how to address this. Hsinchun Chen described research on semantic retrieval and analysis techniques. These advanced 2D and 3D visualization techniques are intended as a way of enabling users to deal with immense quantities of information. Robert Wedgeworth described the legal, technical, and organizational issues that arise in technology transfer. His analysis of the problems encountered and unfortunate misunderstandings, often caused by the novelty of the project, lead to useful insights for the importance of maintaining effective business relationships. Susan Harum explained the process of establishing an effective partnering relationship between the UIUC DLI team members and the publishers who contributed the material, including the crucial issues relating to intellectual property. She also explored the need to market the digital library to its intended end users. Tim Ingoldsby considered the project from the perspective of a publisher (the American Institute of Physics) and what they had gained from the partnership.

The sessions on the final day were intended to provide a broader perspective, moving the discussion out from the UIUC DLI project to future work and issues that arise when one considers the consequences of designing digital libraries and the potential impacts they can have on how people work. Thomas B. Hickey described the work on full-text journals at OCLC over a number of years, explaining the commercial imperatives and their interaction with available technologies. Cathy Marshall explored the use of annotation in physical documents and the implications for the use of digital documents as an exemplar of the importance of considering the wider use of information resources beyond their immediate retrieval. In conlusion, David Levy addressed the extremely broad but crucial issue of acceptability—whether users will want to use the product—and the fears that can arise as the result of the introduction of potentially disruptive new technologies into people's work lives.

Susan Harum and Michael Twidale
Conference Co-Chairs

NSF/DARPA/NASA
DIGITAL LIBRARIES INITIATIVE
A PROGRAM MANAGER'S PERSPECTIVE*

Stephen M. Griffin

INTRODUCTION

The Digital Libraries Initiative (DLI) was the result of a community-based process which began in the late 1980s with informal discussions between researchers and agency program managers. These discussions progressed to planning workshops designed to develop research values and agendas and culminated in the National Science Foundation (NSF)/ Defense Advanced Research Projects Agency (DARPA)/National Aeronautics and Space Administration (NASA) Research in Digital Libraries Initiative announced in late 1993. With the selection and funding of the six DLI projects [http://www.cise.nsf.gov/iis/dli_home.html], interest and activities related to digital libraries accelerated rapidly. The six DLI projects became highly visible and influential efforts and grew in scope, participation, and influence. NSF and DARPA funded additional workshops as part of the DLI to develop consensus on specific digital libraries topical areas and boundaries, to bring together researchers to stimulate cross-disciplinary interaction, and to ponder together how best to adapt to a rapidly changing global information environment. By now, researchers and practitioners from many disciplines have been drawn into digital libraries research and related activities, from subject domains reaching far beyond the sciences into the arts and humanities.

Based on the recognized achievements of DLI and the promise of additional Federal investment in digital libraries, a follow-up program was announced in the spring of 1998. In the new program, "Digital Libraries Initiative—Phase 2," NSF, DARPA, and NASA are joined by the National

*This paper first appeared in *D-Lib Magazine* (July/August 1998), ISSN 1082-9873, <http://www.dlib.org>.

Library of Medicine, the Library of Congress, and the National Endowment for the Humanities as primary sponsors [http://www.nsf.gov/pubs/1998/nsf9863/nsf9863.htm]. First round awards are expected to be made beginning in September 1998.

Digital libraries are meant to provide intellectual access to distributed stores of information by creating information environments which advance access beyond electronic access to raw data—i.e., the bits—to the fuller knowledge and meaning contained in digital collections. Electronic access is increasing at a rapid pace through global efforts to increase network connectivity and bandwidth, new information management tools, and importantly, interoperability across systems and information content. The quantity of online digital information is increasing tenfold each year in a relatively uncontrolled open environment. This pace of information creation far surpasses that of the development of technologies to use the material effectively. The number of people accessing digital collections through the WWW also shows explosive rates of growth. Finally, internationalization is making a "global information environment" a reality. The World Wide Web (WWW) offers a bounty of certain kinds of information to those willing to struggle through the repetitive searching and sifting often required. Digital libraries research is essential to enabling more people to better create and use vast amounts of distributed information and to contribute to the quality and quantity available via the Web and future access frameworks. But it is often not sufficiently appreciated that it is the content that motivates most people to use the Internet and digital libraries. Many Americans and others around the globe are increasingly turning to Internet-based repositories as the primary source of information about many subjects. People of all ages and backgrounds, it turns out, love to browse, explore, and accumulate new knowledge—in short, to learn.

Ultimately, it is the demand for high quality content and ease of access and use that will drive the funding and development of digital libraries. And expectations are high. Users routinely issue 10^1 size queries into 10^{14}+ size data spaces. They look to get the information requested—all of it—but only that which is relevant—and it should take just a few seconds.

Efficient information retrieval— identifying all relevant sources quickly —is one aspect of digital libraries research. Another, and potentially even more valuable, aspect of digital libraries, is their ability to preserve and extend discourse—to provide richer contexts for people to interact with information. The real value of digital libraries may prove to be in their ability to alter the way individuals, groups, organizations, etc., behave, communicate, and conduct their affairs. New forms of collaboration in scholarly and other endeavors are appearing regularly. In this role, digital libraries are powerful instruments of change in social and work practices.

Programmatically, digital libraries remain closely linked to advances in high performance computing and networking and both contribute to and validate these technologies. The merging of advanced computing and communications technologies with massive volumes of digital content will dramatically alter knowledge generation and contexts of use.

DLI AND THE FEDERAL CONTEXT: HPCC

The Digital Libraries Initiative emerged programmatically within the structure of the Federal High Performance Computing and Communications Program (HPCC) [http://www.hpcc.gov/]. HPCC was introduced in a supplementary report to the President's FY1992 Budget and consisted of coordinated efforts in four general focus areas that were executed, for the most part, within established programs in the eight participating agencies. The HPCC Program was the product of several years of planning and discussion within the Federal Coordinating Council for Science, Engineering and Technology (FCCSET). The 1992 report was entitled "Grand Challenges: High Performance Computing and Communications." Grand challenges were driving applications for developing teraflop computing systems and a national high bandwidth network for research and education. The bulk of the program involved funding of high performance computing systems, advanced software technologies and algorithms, and networking infrastructure.

In 1994, the HPCC Program was expanded to include a fifth program component, Information Infrastructure Technology and Applications (IITA). IITA was intended to provide for the research and development needed to develop an underlying technology base for the National Information Infrastructure (NII) and to address National Challenges. National Challenges were seen to be those applications, benefited by HPCC technologies and resources, that could have broad and direct impact on the Nation's competitiveness and the well-being of its citizens. Included in the list of National Challenges were "digital and electronic libraries."

HPCC has evolved into the Federal Computing, Information, and Communications (CIC) programs. The Executive Summary to the FY 1998 Supplement acknowledges the breadth of influence of the Internet and technologies culture of change: "There is little historical precedent for the swift and dramatic growth of the Internet, which, just a few short years ago, was a limited scientific communications network developed by the Government to facilitate cooperation among Federal researchers and the university research community."

The Digital Libraries Initiative is featured prominently in the FY 1998 document as a CIC R&D Highlight, testimony to both its achievements and to the mounting importance of the area generally. This is compelling given that the DLI represents only about 0.6 percent or $6M of the CIC Program's $1100M budget.

A distinctive feature of the continuing Federal computing, information, and communications planning dialogue is a relatively narrow focus on developing technologies for scientific applications and education. Strong reliance is placed on traditional institutional forms, mature disciplinary research communities, and quantitative methodological approaches to problem solving.

DLI PROGRAMMATIC CONTEXT

In the early 1990s, NSF, DARPA and NASA were individually supporting basic research in computing and communications and viewed digital libraries as a broad, newly-emerging topical area of great potential. Informal working groups of agency managers were formed and met regularly over a period of time to define programmatic goals and discuss alternative research agendas. These were, then, the topics of technical workshops funded by the agencies to reconcile with community values and expectations. The reports emanating from the workshops provided the intellectual content of the first program announcement—Research in Digital Libraries—which was released in the fall of 1993. The Digital Libraries Initiative was designed as a basic research initiative to advance the means to collect, store, organize, and access information in digital form via communication networks. Projects were expected to perform high-risk research and to test and demonstrate new technologies.

The program was broadly cast. It was quickly realized, once the proposals were received and reviewed, that DLI needed additional direction and coherence. The 1995 IITA Digital Libraries Workshop entitled "Interoperability, Scaling, and the Digital Library Research Agenda" refined the scope and added coherence to the DLI research agenda. The report coming out of the workshop defined digital libraries as: "An organized collection of multimedia data with information management methods that represent the data as information and knowledge" [http://www.ccic.gov/pubs/iita-dlw/].

The discussions continued as the program evolved. The directions for digital libraries research and benefits of deployment were actively debated within and across technical, library, and other communities. Tensions, some still unresolved, have inhibited interaction and exchange between various communities. An important point of issue is that many see advances in digital libraries research dependent on efforts in domains other than computer and information sciences. The phrase "digital libraries" has been adopted widely over electronic libraries, virtual libraries, and others with the understanding that "electronic" refers primarily to the nature of the technologies which operate on information and "virtual" implies a synthetic environment which resembles the original physical environment. This is as it should be. "Digital" refers to a representation of information on electronic (and other) media. Digital representation adds great potential for enhanced functionality and utility of information corpora. Once information has been digitally encoded, tools and systems can be invented to create altogether new ways to extract meaning from the collection.

Definitions continue to change as researchers and users stretch our thinking about them. The NSF sponsored Santa Fe planning workshop on distributed knowledge work environments [http://www.si.umich.edu/SantaFe/] held in March 1997, broadened the definition of a digital library as follows: "[T]he concept of a 'digital library' is not merely equivalent to a digitized collection with information management tools. It is rather an environment to bring together collections, services, and people in support of the full life cycle of creation, dissemination, use, and preservation of data, information, and knowledge."

The Santa Fe workshop set the intellectual directions and content for Digital Libraries Initiative—Phase 2 (DLI-2). DLI-2 will address a narrower technology research agenda than DLI. Progress to date has suggested areas of greater importance and will support research across the information lifecycle including content creation, access, use and usability, and preservation and archiving. DLI-2 will place emphasis on interoperability and technology integration, content and collection development and management, applications and operational infrastructure, and understanding digital libraries in domain-specific, economic, social, and international contexts—i.e., digital libraries as human-centered systems. The program will go beyond computing and communications specialty communities and proposes to engage scholars, practitioners, and learners with many ambitions including not only science and engineering but also the arts and humanities. By doing so, DLI-2 acknowledges that significant advances in technology will result from the perspectives, methods, and applications of non-science domains—that important new research questions for computer and information sciences will be raised and perhaps answered in venues other than academic computer science research laboratories.

While DLI-2 is part of the Human Centered Systems (HuCS) component of the Federal CIC Programs, its projects are expected to involve content in subject areas across the continuum of human interest. The topical boundaries of DLI-2 activities will be set according to the availability and the character of the sources of program and project investment. DLI-2 also recognizes that collection building and knowledge access are inherently international and will actively promote activities and processes that bridge political and language boundaries. It is hoped that these working groups will provide valuable advice for stimulating international efforts [http://www.si.umich.edu/UMDL/EU_Grant/home.htm].

The new NSF Knowledge and Distributed Intelligence Initiative (KDI) coincides with, and is closely related to DLI-2 [http://www.ehr.nsf.gov/kdi/default.htm]. KDI acknowledges the commonality of approaches in research and development emerging across scientific and engineering disciplines as a result of the deployment of new information technologies and infrastructure. A symposium on KDI was held at the National Academy of Sciences in September 1997 and attended by policy makers and executives from public and private foundations. In calling for the broadest possible dialogue and input, Neal Lane, then director of NSF, stated: "The access we have gained to widely distributed sources of information marks a major accomplishment for human civilization. . . . It is, nevertheless, only a first step. Access to information is one thing. But intelligently absorbing, refining, and analyzing this information to glean useful knowledge is another altogether."

DLI-2 differs from KDI programmatically in that DLI-2 is focused on users and collections—DLI-2 projects are expected to point to future use and usability. Information and processes for delivering information are emphasized across the entire digital libraries life cycle. KDI, particularly the "knowledge networking component," is targeted at fundamental interdisciplinary research about knowledge and knowledge access. While KDI is an NSF-only interdisciplinary program, executed within existing program structures, DLI-2 includes multiple agencies, some which go far beyond interest in science and engineering such as the Library of Congress and the National Endowment for the Humanities. DLI-2 is neutral with respect to subject matter.

DLI PROGRAM CONSTRAINTS

Digital libraries research has not yet gained Federal support commensurate with evident levels of community interest and activity. The supply of research funding falls far short of the demand. Individual agencies continue to be constrained by mission and one year budget cycles. While longer term activities and programs of support have been established, many of these undergo scrutiny on a regular basis—at least every four years with the elections. Digital libraries projects can extend in scope well beyond agency missions and demand support beyond a single agency's means. Larger-scale projects require several years to complete and require a stable and predictable funding stream to retain essential staff and resources.

Research agencies tend to be limited in supporting those research activities and infrastructure building that stay within their defined missions. Maintaining existing disciplinary programs often is favored over beginning true interdisciplinary ones. While encouraging collaboration on the part of performers, it is difficult for sponsors to do the same—to build multiple sponsorship arrangements for single large projects.

Digital libraries projects are typically multi-modal—a mix of research, application, and development of operational systems. It is a fact that some of the most important research issues are bound into the process of building operational systems and analyzing the use and performance of these systems. It is also important that the "libraries" (which may be testbeds or experimental systems) contain collections of value. It is these final two stages of digital libraries research (i.e., what might be considered prototypical operational systems containing content of significant value but still subject to research based on broad-based use) for which it is difficult to find funding from agencies like NSF and DARPA. To achieve a limited expansion of scope, each of the six original DLI projects formed partnerships with various organizations—public (other federal, state, and local governments) and private (major technology vendors, publishers, libraries, schools, etc.). Taken together, over eighty major partnerships were formed which provided the projects with substantially more resources, testing environments, and, importantly, fresh perspectives on their activities. Cost-sharing of more than 100 percent on average was generated. In DLI-2, the challenges are greater still, and agency managers hope that certain selected projects will have sufficient appeal to attract additional funding from other Federal and non-Federal sources.

CONCLUSION

The 1990s are a critical decade when information technology intersects with, and becomes drawn into, endeavors cutting across domain-specific research, education, and commercial and social practices. As a result, many people and organizations are crossing into unfamiliar territory with unpredictable consequences. These are times of enormous opportunity in which decisions made in the present augur prominently in shaping the future. Digital libraries as global multilingual repositories of data, knowledge, sound, and images invite people everywhere to become users and learners.

Digital libraries are inherently international. Knowledge is recorded and stored in many forms, often using different languages and symbol systems. That which exists in one language or located in one country may be only a small part of a corpus of interest. Fuller access to information across language, location, and cultures means fuller understanding of a particular topic and the relationships among topics. Researchers and users must have opportunities to work together if they are to see globally distributed, interoperable, content rich systems. Yet, while scientists and information professionals around the world are engaged in digital libraries research and development, as of now there is little coordination or collaboration because of lack of implementation mechanisms. As part of the Digital Libraries Initiative, a modest step was taken to establish five international working groups to help build DL research agendas for technical, content, social, and economic issues. This effort is jointly funded by the National Science Foundation and the European Union. It is hoped that these working groups will provide valuable advice for international efforts.

There remains an unnatural separation between the producers and consumers of digital libraries resources. A proper balance of attention (and support) among research, applications, content, and collections has yet to be achieved. Localizing research efforts in computer and information sciences venues is limiting, and many believe that efforts in libraries, museums, art departments, schools of music, archeology, history, and other humanities departments are necessary to advance digital libraries research. Yet the science agencies, like NSF, DARPA, and NASA, can only make awards to performers in non-science venues with difficulty—and frequently accompanied by protest from the disciplinary communities normally receiving support from specific agency programs.

DLI benefitted from "bottom-up" program development. It was conceived and planned by program managers at the agencies relying heavily upon community input—not as part of a grander programmatic scheme influenced by transient political value. As such, the monies invested were from the base budgets of the programs involved. (About fifteen separate programs from NSF, DARPA, and NASA contributed funds.) Program managers believed strongly in the values and goals of the initiative—and acted with considerable independence in implementing and executing the program.

By adopting a participatory consensus-based management approach, one that was open, adaptive, and responsive to a larger community, the program was able to be particularly effective in exploiting aspects of the global information infrastructure revolution that was underway. In many ways, the management culture reflected the positive aspects of the open culture of the Internet which the program was attempting to enrich.

The interagency management group for DLI-2, presently composed of managers from the sponsoring agencies, meets regularly to discuss current developments and consider the future. The group adheres to the spirit of DLI management and hopes for broad representation and community involvement and consideration of a large analytical framework to help shape future directions.

UPDATE ON THE NETWORKED DIGITAL LIBRARY OF THESES AND DISSERTATIONS (NDLTD)

Edward A. Fox

INTRODUCTION

The Networked Digital Library of Theses and Dissertations (NDLTD) (http://www.ndltd.org) aims to ensure that all future researchers and scholars have understanding and skills in electronic publishing and have used and submitted a work of their own to a digital library. If all graduate students who are interested in research prepare an electronic thesis or dissertation (ETD) and upload it to NDLTD then electronic publishing and digital libraries will be firmly established in the world of the academy and scholarship. If NDLTD receives proper support, it will become a vast, heterogeneous, federated, multilingual, multimedia digital library with more than 200,000 new works added yearly.

NDLTD is a model digital library project with "something for everyone." Students learn important skills, save money by not having to prepare multiple paper copies, and reach a much larger audience with their theses or dissertations. Universities become involved in work with digital libraries by way of a modest investment of time and resources, which in the long run saves money relative to conventional practices, prepares them for other digital library and electronic publishing projects, and makes their research results more visible and accessible worldwide. Scholars benefit by having a large new collection available with detailed information about university investigations, with known quality, large bibliographies, and careful literature reviews. Digital library enthusiasts have a new collection to experiment with regarding problems in the field (Fox & Sornil, 1999). In subsequent sections, we explore recent progress. For additional information, see the online file of papers and publications at http://www.ndltd.org/pubs/ (NDLTD 1998d).

VISION, BENEFITS, APPROACH, POSSIBILITIES

Graduate education is an important part of the world of higher education in the United States and around the globe (Berelson, 1960). The Council of Graduate Schools (1991) has pinpointed dissertations as playing a key role in the training of researchers; more than 50,000 are completed each year in North America. There are over 350,000 master's degrees awarded yearly in the United States many of which lead to a thesis or substantive report. Hence we adopt the goal for the Networked Digital Library of Theses and Dissertations of collecting at least 200,000 electronic theses or dissertations per year to help improve graduate education (Eaton, Fox, & McMillan, 1997) and extend knowledge sharing on a global level. This will play a role in the move toward a worldwide digital library (Fox & Marchionini, 1998).

The vision behind the Networked Digital Library of Theses and Dissertations is to accomplish multiple objectives through one collaborative effort that will scale to include every university and every graduate student:

- prepare all future scholars for the Information Age (Fox, Hall, & Kipp, 1997) so that they understand important concepts and practices related to electronic publishing, digital libraries, and intellectual property rights, and so the scholarly community will adopt these practices more quickly, smoothly, and effectively;
- help universities to enhance graduate education and to develop expertise regarding digital libraries; and
- build an important digital library that supports scholarship and that improves as a result of new research in the field.

Scalability allows the Networked Digital Library of Theses and Dissertations to expand rapidly and results from:

- having each student, as part of ensuring their education is effective for the Information Age, create their own electronic thesis or dissertation, provide required metadata for it, decide about intellectual property and access rights, and upload it into the digital library;
- having each university run its own part of NDLTD as part of its support for graduate education and its delving into digital libraries;
- applying automation to improve workflow and streamline processing of ETDs so a more efficient scheme results that is cheaper than the old way; and
- federating the various collections and servers in NDLTD so users may view the entire collection as a whole or obtain views based on geography, level, topic, or other criteria.

Other key ideas include:

- demonstrating that, for many purposes, people really can switch fully to electronic documents;
- mandating submission to NDLTD once a university is ready for that step, since then the benefits and collections increase more quickly;
- adopting standards to facilitate preservation and federated access; and
- encouraging universities to work together and share their tools and information, in this domain where competition is minimal while mutual benefit is additive (Fox, 1997, 1998; Fox, Hall, Kipp, Eaton, McMillan, & Mather, 1997).

Since each university can have its own part of the Networked Digital Library of Theses and Dissertations, it is simple to adopt local policies and procedures. In addition, local groups interested in any of the myriad aspects of digital library research can experiment locally to perfect their methods. Thus, at Virginia Tech there are a number of development efforts (Fox, Kipp, & Mather, 1998). These involve applying diverse technologies including OpenText's search system, IBM's digital library product, OCLC's SiteSearch software, a locally developed federated search system (Powell, 1998), and even an experimental system extracting the images in electronic theses and dissertations for display in a virtual reality environment (Bayraktar et al., 1998).

In addition to the goals listed above, it is hoped that the Networked Digital Library of Theses and Dissertations will improve the culture of scholarship. By having a common environment wherein new research is freely shared, there can be greater interchange among students, faculty, and other scholars. Since this environment can be shared worldwide, there can be more understanding internationally and development of larger invisible colleges–all aided through the many tools provided for computer-supported cooperative work. Since universities will support NDLTD locally, it will be possible for undergraduates to connect with research efforts and even to submit their own theses and major papers for inclusion. Finally, all of this may have a profound effect on the world of publishing as universities become more directly involved in the collection and dissemination of research results.

CONCERNS, PROBLEMS, OPPOSITION

On the technical side, there are many digital library problems that relate to improving NDLTD. Since solutions exist or are under development for these, most are discussed in the next section. Here, however, it is appropriate to mention three examples. First, there is the problem of facing the incredibly diverse and fragmented world of electronic publishing, where a myriad of tools, packages, and versions are employed. Somehow one must translate from these to a sensible number of standard forms that can be effectively preserved (Datta & Fox, 1993). This problem, couched in terms of using SGML (Standard Generalized Markup Language, an ISO standard), led to the first workshop about ETDs hosted by UMI in November 1987. Approaching this problem is at the heart of projects that have been called electronic archives (Fox, 1990), electronic libraries and, most recently, digital libraries (Fox, Akscyn, Furuta, & Leggtt, 1995).

Second, there are problems related to cataloging and classifying the contents of digital libraries (McMillan, 1996). One aspect of this concerns standards, too. The Machine-Readable Bibliographic Information Committee (1996) approach leads to the MARC family adopted by many who do cataloging. Recent meetings and activities have led to refinement of a simpler alternative, the Dublin Core, and to crosswalks between it and MARC (Library of Congress, 1997).

Third, there are problems related to searching and accessing a large distributed collection like NDLTD. A closely related problem is that of handling technical reports. This has been examined in the computer science field (Fox, 1995), first through projects like WATERS (French, Fox, Maly, & Selman, 1995), and recently through the Networked Computer Science Technical Report Library (NCSTRL) (Lagoze, 1998). At present, federated searching for ETDs can be handled with a simple system developed at Virginia Tech (NDLTD, 1998a), but more advanced systems will be warranted as the collection expands.

On the social side, there are even more problems that relate to large distributed digital library projects (Borgman, 1996). Since NDLTD calls for widespread change, uses advanced technologies, relates to the Internet and WWW, involves universities and publishers in new relationships, and is emerging at a time of turmoil in the field of scholarly publishing, it has been quite visible in the news (NDLTD, 1998b). Universities are concerned about their expenditures for journals and seek to play a more active role in the process of scholarly publishing (Association of Research Libraries et al., 1998). NDLTD aims to help in this arena, including assisting students, faculty, and universities to understand the issues more thoroughly. Thus it must deal with diverse policies regarding prior publication, derivative works, inclusion of copyrighted materials in ETDs, and tradeoffs among modes of publication (e.g., NDLTD versus journal versus university press). In addition, there are tradeoffs for ETDs regarding collecting, archiving, and accessing—what are the roles of corporations (e.g., UMI), organizations run by libraries (e.g., OCLC), universities, university consortia, and national projects/libraries?

Ultimately, these social issues lead to actions by individuals and universities. Though members of NDLTD (1998c) include supporting organizations and consortia as well as some divisions of universities, most that have joined represent the entire university, so we focus on that group. First, these organizations must identify those interested in the technical, policy, educational, research, and social issues. Volunteers, people assigned, or representatives of the various constituencies (especially the graduate school and library) must join in the local ETD team. Second, there must be discussion on campus so that the general aims of NDLTD can be specialized for the campus. Finally, these ongoing activities must lead to an implementation project that will evolve over the years.

SOLUTIONS, IMPLEMENTATION

With origins dating back to 1987, and with funded research and development led by the NDLTD team at Virginia Tech since 1996, many solutions have emerged. At Virginia Tech, where ETDs have been required since the start of 1997, over 1,100 were in the collection by mid-1998. By that point, there were over 230,000 downloads from around the world of the HTML pages that cover the content of the cover sheet and abstract and almost 200,000 downloads of the full documents.

Handling ETDs is established practice there, supported by staff in the graduate school, library, computing laboratories, and departments. Students carry out their investigations, present their results to their committee in a final defense, complete their ETD, and submit it through a tailored WWW form that captures relevant metadata. The graduate school checks the submission and requests revision until an acceptable form is provided. The library makes the work available through the digital library NDLTD (1998a), also adding cataloging information for the MARC record (which in the 856 field directs people to the online full-text copy) that goes into the campus catalog system.

There is a WWW site for students to help them understand policies and technical issues (NDLTD, 1998f). There are detailed instructions on how to prepare an ETD, explanations of standards and practices related to multimedia and hypermedia, files of questions and answers, templates, and checklists. Most students provide one or more Portable Document Format (PDF) files, while some supply SGML or XML instead; multimedia content is included in supplementary files.

There is an approval form (NDLTD, 1998g) that is printed and goes on file for each ETD to handle the concerns of publishers. It records the decision of the author and faculty committee regarding the breadth of access (e.g., locked up for patent purposes, restricted to campus while awaiting publication in a journal, or open for worldwide downloading). The WWW site includes letters from publishers that allow worldwide ETD access as well as inclusion of derivative articles in their journals. However, students completing the approval form and thinking about other publishers of their results must consult their policies. It is hoped that NDLTD files will record these policies to reduce the need for future inquiries, and more publishers will endorse worldwide access through NDLTD.

NDLTD received funding in September 1996 as a national project (Fox, Eaton, McMillan, Kipp, Weiss, Arce, & Guyer, 1996). Within a year it expanded to an international effort with rapid growth (Fox, Eaton, McMillan, Kipp, Mather, McGonigle, Schweiker, & DeVane, 1997). By summer 1998, thirty-five universities had joined NDLTD. Ongoing efforts to involve more universities will continue to require discussion, visits to campuses, and presentations. Reaching all universities worldwide will take years but should accelerate as larger and more prestigious universities join and a critical mass is achieved.

On the international scene there are promising signs for growth. NDLTD members are on all continents. Groups of universities are joining including three in Canada. Australia has a funded national project involving seven universities. St. Petersburg State Technical University has submitted several proposals for funding to expand efforts in Russia. The National Library of Portugal has joined, and can represent all the universities in the nation. Several universities in Korea and Singapore are members with particular interest in supporting multilingual collections.

Since most graduate studies are carried out in local languages, it is essential that NDLTD include works in all languages and support all fonts. Some groups supporting NDLTD have active research programs in this area (Cao, Lu & Low, 1998; Leong, Cao, & Lu, 1998). These could lead to refinement of the existing federated search system, which uses translation of English query terms through a dictionary database for current multilingual searching (Powell, 1998).

To expand the capabilities of the NDLTD software, a requirements study has been underway in connection with work on an honors thesis. In addition to focus groups and brainstorming in a decision support facility, the effort includes developing and refining a number of scenarios (Carroll, 1995). By spring 1999, there should be a prototype to illustrate the advanced capabilities possible in a digital library focused on aiding graduate students who find, use, and produce electronic theses or dissertations.

CONCLUSION

It is now clear that, eventually, graduate education will shift from more traditional forms to electronic theses or dissertations. Various related projects have emerged (NDLTD, 1998e) and it is hoped will all fit into the broad umbrella of NDLTD. More and more institutions are a part of this federation, and as each develops its own local program, the collection size will grow rapidly.

Issues regarding widespread access and harmonizing with the practices of publishers will remain, since NDLTD aims to effect both change and to extend understanding of policies and practices. Other social concerns will be dealt with by local institutions, the NDLTD Steering Committee, and the implementation team at Virginia Tech as they continue to arise in the normal course of the evolution of this expanding digital library initiative.

On the technical side, ensuring interoperability and preservation, handling a large multilingual collection, and expanding services are key goals. Several proposals for research support have been submitted, and work will continue to deal with the challenges of this model digital library project.

In conclusion, NDLTD has had considerable growth throughout its short history, has dealt with many diverse problems, and has ambitious plans for future activity. It is hoped that new universities will join and contribute not only their ETDs but also share their findings, information, and developments so all can benefit from this broad university collaboration.

ACKNOWLEDGMENTS

Thanks go to the NDLTD Steering Committee, Technical Committee, and Virginia Tech management team (with co-principal investigators John Eaton and Gail McMillan and graduate research assistants Robert Hall, Neill Kipp, Paul Mather, Tim McGonigle). Others helping at Virginia Tech include Emilio Arce, Anthony Atkins, Brian DeVane, Scott Guyer, James Powell, Bill Schweiker, and Laura Weiss. Thanks also go to all the members of NDLTD and their faculty, staff, and students.

Funding has been provided by the Southeastern Universities Research Association and the U.S. Department of Education (FIPSE). Donations have been given by IBM, Adobe, Microsoft, OCLC, and others. Support and in-kind contributions have been given by many groups including the Coalition for Networked Information, Conference of Southern Graduate Schools, Council of Graduate Schools, and SOLINET (SOutheastern LIbrary NETwork).

REFERENCES

Association of Research Libraries, Association of American Universities, & Pew Higher Education Roundtable. (1998). To publish and perish. *Policy Perspectives* [special issue], 7(4), 1-11.

Bayraktar, M.; Zhang, C.; Vadapalli, B.; Kipp, N.; & Fox, E. A. (1998). A Web art gallery. In *Proceedings of the Third ACM Conference on Digital Libraries, DL '98* (Pittsburgh, PA, June 23-26, 1998) (pp. 277-278). New York: ACM Press.

Berelson, B. (1960). *Graduate education in the United States.* New York: McGraw-Hill.

Borgman, C. (Ed.). (1996). *Social aspects of digital libraries* (A workshop hosted by UCLA, sponsored by NSF, February 16-17, 1996, UCLA, CA). Retrieved September 17, 1999 from the World Wide Web: http://www-lis.gseis.ucla.edu/DL/.

Cao, L.; Leong, M. K.; Lu, Y.; & Low, H. B. (1998). Searching heterogeneous multilingual bibliographic sources. *Computer Networks and ISDN Systems, 30*(1-7), 612-615.

Carroll, J. M. (Ed.). (1995). *Scenario-based design: Envisioning work and technology in system development.* New York: John Wiley & Sons.

Council of Graduate Schools. (1991). *The role and nature of the doctoral dissertation: A policy statement.* Washington, DC: Council of Graduate Schools.

Dalal, K., & Fox, E. A. (1993). *Document translation: Dissertations and technical reports.* Unpublished Technical Report TR-93-31, Department of Computer Science, Virginia Tech, Blacksburg, VA.

Eaton, J.; Fox, E. A.; & McMillan, G. (1997). Electronic Theses and Dissertations (ETDs) and their contribution to graduate education. In *Proceedings of the 53rd Annual Meeting Midwestern Association of Graduate Schools, MAGS* (pp. 73-78). Chicago: MAGS.

Fox, E. A. (1990). How to proceed toward electronic archives and publishing. *Psychological Science, 1*(6), 355-358.

Fox, E. A. (1995). World-Wide Web and computer science reports. *Communications of the ACM, 38*(4), 43-44.

Fox, E. A. (1997). Networked Digital Library of Theses and Dissertations: An international collaboration promoting scholarship. *ICSTI Forum, Quarterly Newsletter of the International Council for Scientific and Technical Information* (No. 26) 8-9 November. Retrieved September 17, 1999 from the World Wide Web: http://www.icsti.nrc.ca/icsti/.

Fox, E. A. (1998). Networked digital library of theses and dissertations: A framework for east-west collaboration. In *Proceedings of Asian Digital Library Workshop, "East Meets West"* (5-7 August 1998, Hong Kong, hosted by University of Hong Kong). Retrieved September 17, 1999 from the World Wide Web: http://www.ndltd.org/pubs/Asia98.htm.

Fox, E. A.; Akscyn, R.; Furuta, R.; & Leggett, J. (1995). Guest editors' introduction to digital libraries. *Communications of the ACM, 38*(4), 22-28.

Fox, E. A.; Eaton, J.; McMillan, G.; Kipp, N.; Weiss, L.; Arce, E.; & Guyer, S. (1996). National Digital Library of Theses and Dissertations: A scalable and sustainable approach to unlock university resources. *D-Lib Magazine*, September. Retrieved September 17, 1999 from the World Wide Web: http://www.dlib.org/dlib/september96/theses/09fox.html.

Fox, E. A.; Eaton, J.; McMillan, G.; Kipp, N.; Mather, P.; McGonigle, T.; Schweiker, W.; & DeVane, B. (1997). Networked Digital Library of Theses and Dissertations: An international effort unlocking university resources. *D-Lib Magazine*, September. Retrieved September 17, 1999 from the World Wide Web: http://www.dlib.org/dlib/september97/theses/09fox.html.

Fox, E. A.; Hall, R.; & Kipp, N. (1997). NDLTD: Preparing the next generation of scholars for the information age. *New Review of Information Networking (NRIN), 3,* 59-76.

Fox, E. A.; Hall, R.; Kipp, N.; Eaton, J. L.; McMillan, G.; & Mather, P. (1997). NDLTD: Encouraging international collaboration in the academy. *DESIDOC Bulletin of Information Technology, 17*(6), 45-56.

Fox, E. A.; Kipp, N.; & Mather, P. (1998). How digital libraries will save civilization. *Database Programming & Design, 12*(8).

Fox, E. A., & Marchionini, G. (1998). Toward a worldwide digital library: Introduction. *Communications of the ACM, 41*(4), 28-32.

Fox, E. A., & Sornil, O. (1999). Digital libraries. In R. Baeza-Yates & B. Ribeiro-Neto (Eds.), *Modern information retrieval* (pp. 415-432). New York: ACM Press.

French, J.; Fox, E. A.; Maly, K.; & Selman, A. (1995). Wide area technical report service—technical reports online. *Communications of the ACM, 38*(4), 45.

Lagoze, C. (1998). *NCSTRL Home Page.* Retrieved September 17, 1999 from the World Wide Web: http://www.ncstrl.org.

Leong, M. K.; Cao, L.; & Lu, Y. (1998). Distributed Chinese bibliographic searching. *Communications of the ACM, 41*(4), 66-68.

Library of Congress. (1997). Metadata, Dublin Core and USMARC: A review of current efforts (MARBI Discussion Paper no. 99, January). Retrieved September 17, 1999 from the World Wide Web: gopher://marvel.loc.gov/00/.listarch/usmarc/dp99.doc.

Machine-Readable Bibliographic Information Committee. (1996). *The USMARC Formats: Background and principles* (Machine-Readable Bibliographic Information Committee in conjunction with Network Development and MARC Standards Office, November).

Retrieved September 17, 1999 from the World Wide Web: http://lcweb.loc.gov/marc/96principl.html.

McMillan, G. (1996). Electronic theses and dissertations: Merging perspectives. *Cataloging and Classification Quarterly, 22*(3/4), 105-125.

NDLTD. (1998a). *ETD Digital Library.* Retrieved September 17, 1999 from the World Wide Web: http://www.theses.org.

NDLTD. (1998b). *NDLTD in the News.* Retrieved September 17, 1999 from the World Wide Web: http://www.ndltd.org/news/

NDLTD. (1998c). *NDLTD Official Members.* Retrieved September 17, 1999 from the World Wide Web: http://www.ndltd.org/contacts/.

NDLTD. (1998d). *NDLTD Papers and Publications.* Retrieved September 17, 1999 from the World Wide Web: http://www.ndltd.org/pubs/.

NDLTD. (1998e). *NDLTD Related Projects.* Retrieved September 17, 1999 from the World Wide Web: http://www.ndltd.org/related/projects.htm.

NDLTD. (1998f). *Virginia Tech Electronic Thesis and Dissertation home page.* Retrieved September 17, 1999 from the World Wide Web: http://etd.vt.edu/.

NDLTD. (1998g). *Virginia Tech Graduate School Electronic Submission Approval Form.* Retrieved September 17, 1999 from the World Wide Web: http://etd.vt.edu/submit/approval.htm.

Powell, J. (1998). *Virginia Tech federated searcher.* Retrieved September 17, 1999 from the World Wide Web: http://jin.dis.vt.edu/fedsearch/. Also used for *Networked Digital Library of Theses and Dissertations: Federated search.* Retrieved September 17, 1999 from the World Wide Web: http://www.theses.org.

Processing and Access Issues for Full-Text Journals

William H. Mischo and Timothy W. Cole

INTRODUCTION

The University of Illinois at Urbana-Champaign (UIUC) was one of six sites awarded a four-year federally funded grant in 1994 under the first phase of the Digital Library Initiative (DLI). The DLI grants, jointly funded by the National Science Foundation (NSF), the Defense Advanced Research Project Agency (DARPA), and the National Aeronautics and Space Administration (NASA), were awarded, in addition to UIUC, to Stanford University, the University of California at Berkeley, Carnegie Mellon University, the University of California at Santa Barbara, and the University of Michigan. A detailed description of the Illinois DLI project, along with links to the other five projects, can be found at http://dli.grainger.uiuc.edu/ and is described in Schatz et al. (1999) and Schatz et al. (1996).

Activities on the $4 million UIUC DLI grant have been carried out by a multi-departmental research team comprised of individuals from the university's Graduate School of Library and Information Science, the University Library, the National Center for Supercomputing Applications (NCSA), and the Department of Computer Science. The project also includes important in-kind contributions in the form of full-text articles in SGML format from a number of professional society publishers and significant equipment and software grants from several companies. The Illinois DLI project includes research, testbed, and evaluation components.

This article will describe the design and implementation of the Illinois DLI testbed. It will focus on the issues addressed, the problems encountered, and the lessons learned in the course of deploying the testbed. This work was carried out by the testbed team headquartered in the Grainger Engineering Library Information Center, a $22 million facility that opened in 1994 and is dedicated to the exploration of emerging information technologies.

The testbed is constructed from source text journal articles in the areas of engineering, physics, and computer science contributed by several professional society publishers. This contributed testbed source material is comprised of full-text articles in SGML format and bit-mapped images of figures of sixty-three journal titles presently containing over 60,000 articles from 1995 forward. The full-text articles for the testbed have been contributed by the American Institute of Physics (AIP), the American Physical Society (APS), the American Society of Civil Engineers (ASCE), the Institute of Electrical and Electronics Engineers Computer Society (IEEE CS), and the Institution of Electrical Engineers (IEE). Several other publisher collections were examined but not included in the testbed.

TESTBED GOALS AND ISSUES

The overarching focus of the DLI testbed team has been on the design, development, and evaluation of mechanisms that can provide effective access to full-text engineering, physics, and computer science journal articles within an Internet environment. The primary goals of the Illinois testbed have been:

1. the construction and testing of a scalable multi-publisher heterogeneous SGML-based full-text testbed employing flexible search and rendering capabilities and offering extensive links to local and remote information resources;
2. the development of procedures for the local processing, indexing, normalization (through use of metadata), retrieval, and rendering of full-text journal literature in marked-up format as provided by contributing publishers;
3. the integration of the testbed (and other full-text resources) into the continuum of information resources offered to end-users by the library system;
4. determining the efficacy of full-text article searching vis-à-vis document surrogate searching, and exploring end-user full-text searching behavior in an attempt to identify user-searching needs; and
5. identifying models for the effective publishing and retrieval of full-text articles within an Internet environment and employing these models in the testbed design and development.

On an overarching level, the project has addressed the issues connected with the migration from a print-based journal collection to an Internet-based model. The testbed team has identified the staff and hardware requirements necessary for the local processing, loading, and retrieval of full-text data. In addition, the team has generated mechanisms for providing access (via links) to testbed materials and other publisher repositories through standard retrieval tools such as Abstracting and Indexing (A & I) services. Both of these approaches focus on defining retrieval mechanisms to optimize user access to full-text journals.

At the onset of the DLI Project, the testbed team faced a number of clearly defined design and development issues. These issues related to collection procurement and utility, the identification of standards for the format of the collection materials, accurate rendering of materials, the development of processing procedures, optimum database search engine retrieval capabilities, and the determination of the appropriate mix of off-the-shelf software versus locally developed code.

All full-text retrieval test systems face limitations relating to the breadth and the depth of the collection. Test systems cannot typically include all the subject-related journals needed to meet the needs of researchers in the covered discipline. Likewise, the typical full-text test collections will not provide the years of coverage necessary to completely meet the needs of researchers. (Interestingly, these two problems have been made more acute by the discrete publisher-based full-text retrieval system model we see today.) The Illinois testbed, comprised of sixty-three journals, has addressed these issues through expanded links from full-text references and by providing simultaneous searching of testbed resources and A & I service databases. The integration of distributed full-text repositories will continue to be addressed within the testbed.

When work on the UIUC DLI project began in 1994, the World Wide Web (WWW) was in a nascent stage. At that time, NCSA's Mosaic 2.0 beta was the browser of choice, the HTML 2.0 standard was still under development, Netscape had yet to release its first Web browser, and Microsoft Windows 3.1 was the standard PC operating system. Early studies of the effectiveness of full-text retrieval were necessarily limited in scope, primarily because of the breadth/depth problem and the lack of figures, mathematics, and tables for the article display (Tenopir & Ro, 1990).

The initial task of the testbed project team was to identify technologies that were both of sufficient maturity to be usable at once and of sufficient potential to evolve over the life of the project. As the project evolved, two clear trends emerged: the WWW has become the standard for text retrieval and display and, as a direct corollary, publishers have taken advantage of emerging Web technologies to establish their own full-text repositories.

TESTBED TECHNOLOGIES:
SGML FORMAT AND RENDERING

Critical to the ultimate success of the project was the determination of the testbed document format standard. The ideal format would support full-text indexing; high-granularity field-specific search and retrieval; and robust platform-independent rendering. No existing format matched all criteria, and it was immediately obvious that HTML 2.0 fell far short of desired structure and rendering functionality. The Standard Generalized Markup Language (SGML), a nonproprietary international standard, was clearly the best of the formats available for exposing the intellectual content and structure of documents. The Text Encoding Initiative (TEI) (Sperberg-McQueen, 1994) was built around SGML, and pilot full-text journal publishing projects using SGML were then underway at OCLC (Weibel, 1994). However, rendering engines for SGML were limited and required separate executables or plug-ins.

Two other contending document formats were also examined. TeX and LaTeX are well established in the mathematical sciences academic community and support extremely robust rendering of mathematics, but the available authoring and display tools were limited and were largely UNIX-based. Also, exposure of document structure in TeX as used in real-world applications is limited.

PDF, an Adobe-proprietary format, provided the best emulation of the printed page. Adobe Acrobat reader was free and available for multiple platforms. However, PDF lacked (as of 1994) important hyperlink functionality and vital (for our project) cross-collection indexing features. It also was then, and remains today, a primarily appearance-oriented format.

SGML was chosen for the testbed document format standard because it was nonproprietary and inherently best both for indexing and for search and retrieval. This decision was consistent with the publishing world's identification of SGML as the emerging standard for document representation and transmission. While all publishers contributing source materials for the project had experience with the three formats under consideration, it was clear that SGML or SGML with embedded TeX for mathematical equations was the preferred format.

However, the use of SGML in a Web environment presents some formidable challenges. The lack of suitable SGML renderers has hindered the project from the very beginning. It was the hope of the testbed team that, as the technologies evolved, there would be advances in SGML rendering engines, but these improvements have not materialized. To compensate for immediate SGML rendering limitations, several of the publishers provided PDF versions of articles in addition to SGML versions. Figure 1 shows an excerpt of a sample article in PDF format displayed by Adobe Acrobat. Figure 2 shows the same article excerpt in SGML format rendered by the SoftQuad Panorama viewer. Note that the Panorama SGML viewer has problems with the accurate rendering of display mathematics, in particular with kerning operations, fraction bars, radical length, and line breaks. Note also that PDF rendering imitates the published page layout while the SGML rendering results in a less structured and continuous display.

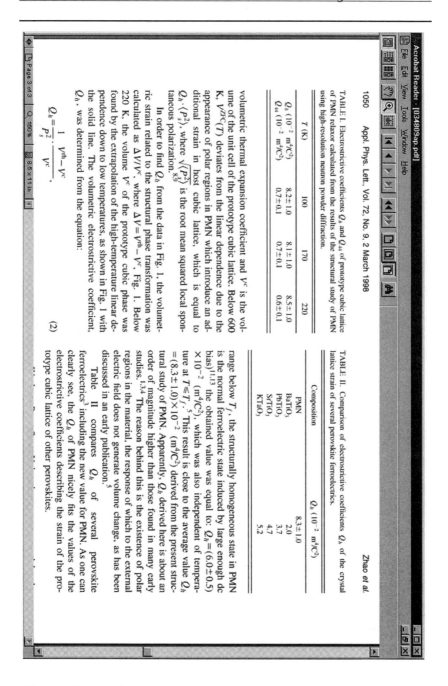

Figure 1. Excerpt from Testbed Article as Rendered in Adobe Acrobat Reader
(PDF Format)

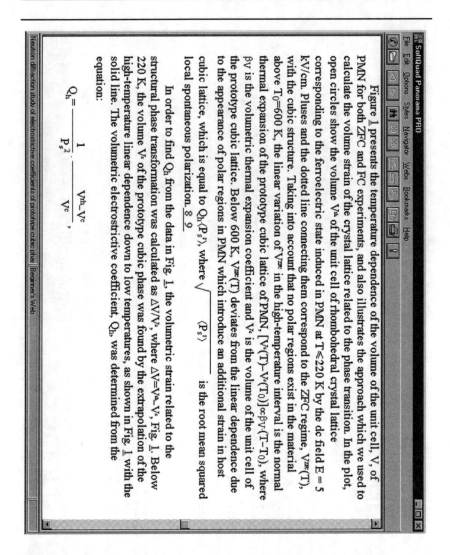

Figure 2. Excerpt from Testbed Article as Rendered in SoftQuad Panorama Viewer, Version 2.0 (SGML Format)

The most problematic aspect of SGML full-text rendering has been in accurately rendering SGML display mathematics. One of the exciting promises of marked-up mathematics is in the potential for searching and displaying both syntactic and semantic elements of article mathematics. The testbed team has explored several techniques for rendering mathematics in a Web-based environment, including converting SGML display mathematics to TeX (and subsequently bit-mapped images) and also the display of marked-up mathematics within HTML and XML using Cascading Style Sheets (CSS). The accurate rendering of mathematics continues to be a major focus of attention for scientific publishing on the Web. The testbed team is experimenting with search techniques for marked-up mathematics.

SGML is an open standard for document representation and transmission. However, SGML is not in itself a markup language but rather a template or model for marking up the content and structure of a document. The Document Type Definition (DTD) accompanying an individual publisher's SGML is the instrument that actually specifies the semantics and syntax of the tags to be used in the document markup. The DTD also specifies the rules that describe the manner in which the SGML tags may be applied to the documents. One of the major roadblocks in the successful deployment of the testbed has been the overhead involved with processing the heterogeneous DTDs of the publishers. Each publisher DTD has required its own suite of processing software. In the process of creating a viable testbed, the Illinois testbed team developed a number of techniques to address problems and normalize SGML processing, indexing, storage, retrieval, and rendering.

The testbed team has converted the SGML publisher data into well-formed XML (eXtensible Markup Language). The XML data can then be rendered natively (without conversion) in a Web browser and/or converted to HTML to be rendered using emerging Web technologies such as CSS and Dynamic HTML (DHTML). It is clear that a rich markup format such as XML, which is a nearly complete instance of SGML, will become the standard language of open document systems, to be used in Web environments for document representation and delivery. XML and SGML permit documents to be treated as objects to be viewed, manipulated, and output. The major strengths of these markup languages, in terms of their retrieval capabilities, are their ability to reveal the deep content and structure of a document. While SGML and XML are becoming ubiquitous in the publishing world, they are still, for the most part, being generated by publishers as a byproduct for archiving and search engine indexing, rather than serving as an integral, integrated part of the production process.

SGML, HTML, and XML, for document representation and display, offer various levels of maturity. SGML supports powerful indexing, search, and retrieval but requires a sophisticated search engine and a plug-in viewer for display. SGML is generally regarded as difficult to use and, along with the client, delivery, and rendering issues, remains a "Web-unfriendly" technology. HTML is ubiquitous and with HTML 4.0 and CSS provides robust rendering capabilities. However, HTML remains a presentation-oriented language with inadequate semantic tools for the effective indexing and fine-granularity searching needed for academic journals. XML is a distinguished subset of SGML that retains the key features of SGML, including semantic-based tagging. But, XML and the XSL styling language are new technologies still being shaped by the standards process. XML cannot be rendered accurately in the 4.0 browsers but is easy to transform to HTML and can be natively rendered by Internet Explorer 5.0.

Figures 3 and 4 show HTML and XML renderings of the same article excerpt displayed in Figures 1 and 2. Note that the use of CSS provides enhanced mathematics rendering and promises sophisticated display capabilities.

DATABASE SEARCH ENGINES AND ARTICLE SERVERS

Various database management systems capable of indexing and searching SGML-based databases were examined. The OpenText DBMS was chosen for the testbed because of its ability to exploit the strengths of SGML. The OpenText search engine grew out of work done at the University of Waterloo to create and index the SGML version of the Oxford English Dictionary (Terry, 1991). OpenText also had attractive features for indexing document metadata in conjunction with document full-text, for normalizing documents created with different publisher Document Type Definitions (DTDs), and for maintaining multiple discrete database repositories. Additionally, OpenText's architecture allows the integration of third party tools, the implementation of locally developed scripts and code, the capability of bypassing unneeded component modules, and the ability to rapidly change processing procedures in response to dynamic processing needs.

Originally the UIUC DLI project had expected to influence generic Web client development by influencing development of the NCSA Mosaic Web browser. This proved a naïve expectation. The testbed team realized that search and delivery of testbed materials needed to be done in a browser-neutral manner. A focus of the testbed project has been the development of server-side scripts and dynamic document merge capabilities. The testbed team has employed NT and UNIX operating system platforms as appropriate to task. Netscape Enterprise and Microsoft Internet Information Server Web servers are used. Web server functionality is extended using both conventional CGI and more advanced techniques such as Microsoft's Active Server Platform (ASP). HTTPS protocols (HTTP with

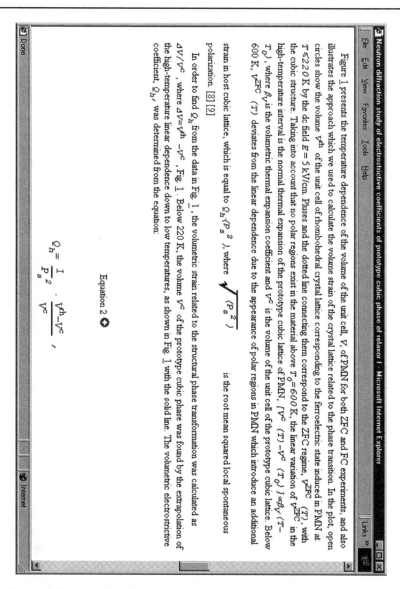

Figure 3. Excerpt from Testbed Article as Rendered in Microsoft Internet Explorer, Version 5.0 (HTML Format)

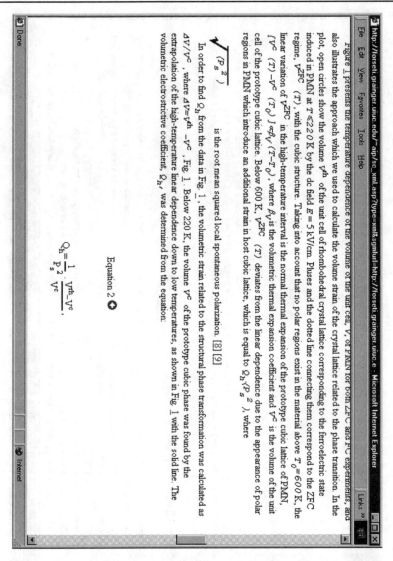

Figure 4. Excerpt from Testbed Article as Rendered in Microsoft Internet Explorer, Version 5.0 (XML Format)

Secure Socket Layers) are used for user authentication and authorization as required. HTTP protocols are used for all other interactions with clients.

The testbed team has implemented a large-scale Web-based testbed of full-text journal articles featuring enhanced access and display capabilities. The Web-based retrieval system developed by the DLI testbed and evaluation teams is called DeLIver (Desktop Link to Virtual Engineering Resources). The DeLIver client, which replaced a Microsoft Windows-based custom client in use for the first two years of the project, has been in operation since September 1997 and is being used by over 2,000 registered UIUC students and faculty and also designated outside researchers. Figure 5 shows the DeLIver search interface. Figure 6 shows an abbreviated citation results list and Figure 7 the extended citation for a specific retrieved item. The contents of the display shown in Figure 7 represents the metadata associated with the retrieved item. Detailed transaction log data of user search sessions (gathered and merged from both database and Web servers) are being kept, and a preliminary analysis of user search patterns from some 4,200 search sessions has been performed.

TESTBED PROCESSING

Figure 8 shows the processing flow for the testbed. Materials are received from publishers and distributed to in-house repository document servers. Pre-processing scripts are run to embed links to associated figures, check character entities, and extract and create a metadata file for each document (using RDF syntax and Dublin Core semantics supplemented with project-specific elements) (W3C: World Wide Web Consortium, 1999; The Dublin Core Metadata Initiative, 1998). Metadata is heavily used in the testbed both to normalize searching and to maintain link information between objects (articles) in the testbed and related objects (articles, A & I service records, and so on) external to the testbed. The project-specific metadata semantics go well beyond the minimal metadata tagging semantics of the Dublin Core and similar schema designed for general use on the Web.

OpenText indexes are then built. The article metadata is indexed along with the full-text of the articles. The individual indexes can be searched separately or in parallel. Tag aliasing is applied to support normalized searching. CGI and ASP scripts are used to enhance search functionality; insert hyperlink information; perform transformations between SGML, XML, and HTML formats; and facilitate linking between testbed objects and related information both within, and external to, the testbed.

RETRIEVAL MODELS

To support effective retrieval in the testbed, the Illinois DLI testbed

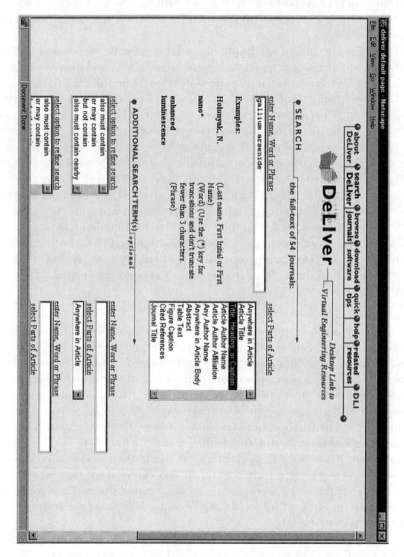

Figure 5. Illinois DLI Search Interface Screen Showing Variety of Article
Elements that can be Searched

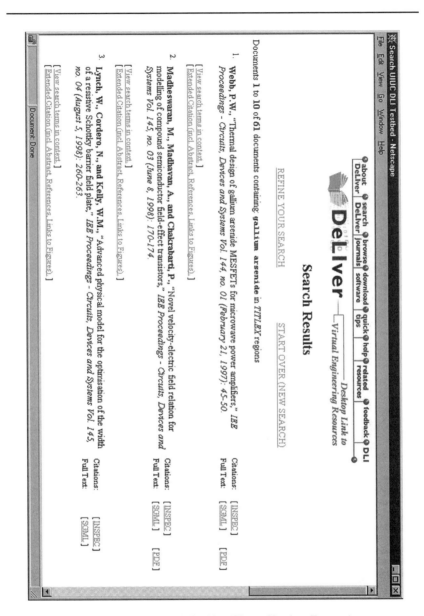

Figure 6. Search Results List (Short Citation Format)

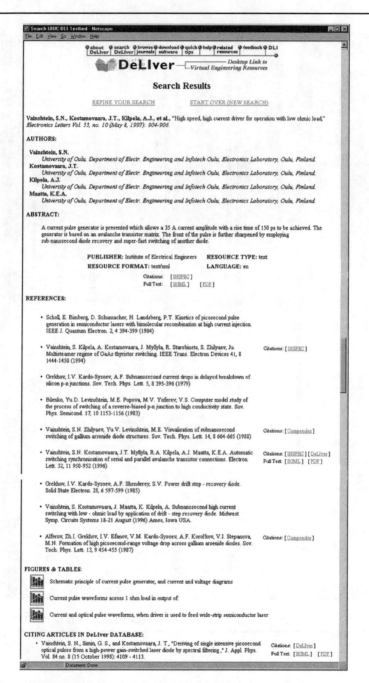

Figure 7. Extended Citation for Testbed Article; Item Metadata is Used to Create this View

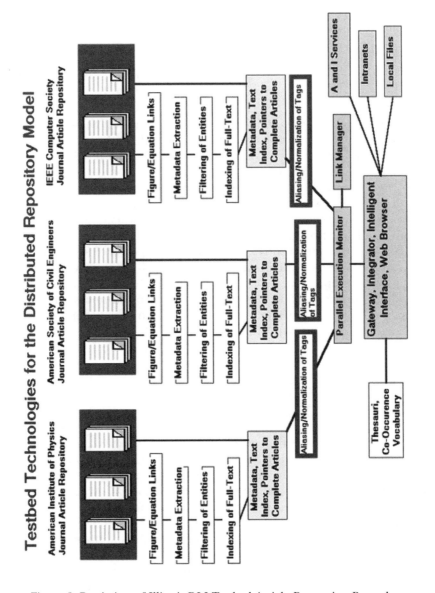

Figure 8. Depiction of Illinois DLI Testbed Article Processing Procedures

and evaluation teams have also carried out studies of end-user searching behavior in an attempt to identify user-searching needs. One requirement specified by the testbed team from the onset of the project has been that the testbed (as a resource for users) must be integrated into the continuum of information resources offered by the library system. This has been addressed by providing access to the testbed in two ways: (1) by making the testbed DeLIver system a search option within the library public terminal top-level menu; and (2) by linking testbed full-text records from the short entry displays within the Ovid Compendex and INSPEC periodical index databases. Additional simultaneous search mechanisms and standards (including Z39.50) are being implemented, including the ability to search DeLIver and selected periodical indexes from a single client screen.

The cornerstones of the testbed, in terms of its retrieval capabilities, are the exposed article content and structure revealed by SGML and the associated article-level metadata, which serves to normalize the heterogeneous SGML and provide short-entry display capability. The metadata also contain links to internal and external data, such as forward and backward links to other testbed articles and links to A & I service databases and other full-text repositories, such as the American Institute of Physics and the American Physical Society sites for PDF format documents and titles outside the testbed. An important feature of the testbed design is the separation of the metadata/index files from the full-text. This allows the metadata/index—containing pointers to the full-text—to be logically and physically separated from the full-text records.

An important concern of the testbed group has been in exploring effective retrieval models for the evolving Web-based electronic journal publishing system. The retrieval and display of full-text journal literature in an Internet environment poses a number of issues for both publishers and libraries. It has now become commonplace for publishers to provide Internet (Web-based) access to the electronic versions of their publications with particular focus on journal issues and articles. For academic libraries, support for this publisher-based online journal environment introduces new levels of budgeting concerns and involves an examination of library collection policies, user access mechanisms, networking capabilities, archiving policies, availability of proper equipment, and a greater awareness of requisite licensing agreements.

Libraries have not historically structured information retrieval services around discrete publisher repository collections. There is a need for creative mechanisms to provide effective search and retrieval across the burgeoning number of distributed heterogeneous publisher repositories. To support this, the testbed team has proposed a distributed repository model that "federates" or connects the individual publisher repositories of full-text documents. In the DLI testbed model, these distributed repositories are federated by the extraction of normalized metadata, index, and link data from the heterogeneous full text of the different publishers. This model addresses the challenge of providing standardized and consistent search capabilities across these distributed and disparate repositories.

The testbed team has succeeded in demonstrating the efficacy of the distributed repository model by producing cross-DTD metadata, providing parallel database querying and retrieval techniques across a distinguished subset of the full-text repositories, and by establishing and accessing an off-site repository at a publisher's location.

ACCOMPLISHMENTS

In the four years of the grant, the testbed team has developed a number of features and technologies for the testbed. The testbed team has focused on developing technologies for the effective building of local repositories and also the complementary task of providing mechanisms for integrating distributed repositories and other resources. In summary, the testbed team has been responsible for:

1. the development of a metadata specification to support standardized retrieval across repositories; short-entry display independent of the discrete full-text document repositories; and links to associated testbed items, A & I service databases, and other repositories;
2. the development of an SGML tag aliasing or normalization system to accommodate heterogeneous DTDs;
3. the development of the Web DeLIver and custom Windows clients for search, retrieval, and display across multiple discrete repositories;
4. providing, from within the above clients, cross-repository retrieval from single search command arguments;
5. addressing issues connected with the rendering of SGML within the Softquad Panorama viewer;
6. addressing issues connected with rendering mathematics (an international mathematics rendering conference was organized and held at the Grainger Library in 1996);
7. deploying enhanced retrieval mechanisms, such as Author Word Wheels and enhanced link mechanisms, in a Web-based environment;
8. developing an Ovid INSPEC and Compendex proxy with links to the DeLIver testbed and other remote publisher repositories;
9. providing links from the bibliographies of retrieved DeLIver article extended citations to other articles contained in the testbed;
10. providing forward citation links within testbed article extended citations to subsequently published articles that cite the retrieved testbed article;
11. providing links from the retrieved DeLIver articles and references in the bibliographies of retrieved DeLIver articles to INSPEC,

Compendex, SPIN, and other records in periodical index and repositories systems;

12. employing Web-based user questionnaires and surveys;
13. generating detailed user transaction logs, gathered at the search argument level, with the automatic identification and storage of characteristics of each user search sessions;
14. providing in-depth analysis of user search behavior, including statistics on the frequency of use of each DeLIver search feature;
15. providing simultaneous searching of a user entered search argument in DeLIver and periodical index databases;
16. employing a Web-Kerberos based user authentication via the UIUC Bluestem Web-based user authentication system (Cole, 1997); and
17. testing the capability of digital signing of documents.

This work has been accomplished with the cooperation and support of our publisher partners and through the use of commercial software from OpenText, Hewlett-Packard, SoftQuad, and Microsoft. The testbed team has made available the results of the project to our publisher partners and sponsors in annual workshops and through regular communications.

LESSONS LEARNED

The potential of SGML (and now XML) has been borne out by experience. The full-text indexes are extremely rich, supporting a measure of search precision unavailable in previous full-text search systems. Figure 5 shows the search fields available to end-users in the current interface. SGML has greatly facilitated extraction of metadata and insertion of hyperlinks to related resources within and external to the testbed.

Rendering of complex mathematical mark-up continues to be problematic. Until recently the testbed relied solely on the Panorama SGML viewer originally marketed by SoftQuad. In spite of promises to improve the rendering engine, development has lagged (Panorama was recently sold to Interleaf) and there still isn't a version of Panorama for the Macintosh. Rapid development of XML, advances in the latest version of HTML, and development of Cascading Style Sheets (CSS) are improving prospects for better rendering. Nonetheless, our experience with Panorama demonstrates the degree to which libraries and information providers are dependent on the commercial sector for essential technology.

A detailed transaction log analysis of 4,158 end-user search sessions has been conducted. Several interesting results have been gleaned from the transaction logs. These include: there is very little use being made of either "Help" or "Quicktips" functions; browsing of tables of contents is being performed in 39 percent of the search sessions; full-text searching is the predominant search mode, but in 24 percent of the sessions users performed a search within a specific field; full-text is displayed in more sessions (69 percent) than extended citations (19 percent); in 25 percent of the sessions, users did multi-concept searching; and an average of four full-text documents are viewed per session.

Overall development of the testbed has taken longer than anticipated. With some notable exceptions—e.g., the lack of a robust SGML viewer—the technology needed has been available by the time needed. The development of processing procedures, the normalization of DTDs, and the development and implementation of metadata semantics have taken longer than anticipated. Technology infrastructure changes happen much more quickly than process changes that involve changing how libraries and information providers do their jobs.

Implementation of a digital information resource requires tighter integration of the parties involved. Small changes by a publisher in tagging semantics can require corresponding changes in indexing scripts, metadata extraction procedures and, further downstream, style sheet design. Conversely, changes in browser software or rendering client can necessitate changes in tagging and indexing. Because each of these tasks may be performed by a different agency, close efficient working relationships are essential.

In the electronic journal environment, roles and responsibilities are more fluid. While documents may reside on a publisher's server, metadata may reside elsewhere—e.g., on an abstracting and indexing service's hardware. Different agencies may create different metadata for the same objects—e.g., using different controlled vocabularies. Libraries may implement their own gateways and portals or may contract for such services with consortia or other third parties. A single article may be found through different gateways, using different index and metadata providers, even if full content of the article itself still comes from a single publisher's server. Archival responsibilities may be distributed among libraries, consortia, and publishers.

In the rapidly evolving electronic journals environment, academic libraries will need to re-examine their collection development policies in terms of ownership versus access, become more actively involved in institutional and consortial licensing agreements, and become more actively involved in campus networking, server, and workstation policies and technologies.

FUTURE FOCI

The testbed team expects to continue work on the issues addressed in the DLI grant through a Corporation for National Research Initiatives (CNRI) grant and the establishment of a Collaborating Partners program. CNRI has established a collaborative Digital Library (D-Lib) Test Suite program encompassing five operational digital library testbeds. The D-Lib Test Suite program is expected to provide a fertile research environment for the information science community. The testbed team members and associated researchers will explore a number of evolving information technologies.

The entire testbed was recently converted to XML. Testbed articles are now retrievable in XML and HTML as well as in PDF and SGML. This has already improved rendering options and overall quality. The potential of the Math ML standard to support more accurate rendering of testbed content will be investigated (W3C: World Wide Web Consortium, 1999).

In addition, further testing of distributed architecture models will be done to test scalability and performance of the options. The use of Document Object Identifiers (DOIs) ("Technology Update: Digital Object Identifiers," 1998) and other emerging standards to enhance and facilitate link management will be investigated.

Also, additional simultaneous search features—e.g., allowing simultaneous searching of non-testbed information resources—will be further refined. It is expected that search agent technologies, including Knowbot software, will play an important role in the evolving distributed repository model being promoted by the Illinois testbed.

REFERENCES

Cole, T. (1997). Using Bluestem for Web user authentification and access control of library resources. *Library Hi-Tech, 15*(1-2), 58-71.

Dublin Core Metadata Initiative. (1998). *The Dublin Core: A simple content description model for electronic resources* [online]. Retrieved January 24, 2000 from the World Wide Web: http://purl.oclc.org/dc/.

Schatz, B.; Mischo, W. H.; Cole, T. W.; Bishop, A.; Harum, S.; Johnson, E.; Neumann, L.; & Chen, H. (1999). Federated search of scientific literature: A retrospective on the Illinois Digital Library Project. *IEEE Computer, 32*(2), 51-59.

Schatz, B.; Mischo, W. H.; Cole, T. W.; Hardin, J.; Bishop, A.; & Chen, H. (1996). Federating diverse collections of scientific literature. *IEEE Computer, 29*(5), 28-37.

Sperberg-McQueen, C. M. (1994). The Text Encoding Initiative: Electronic text markup for research. In B. Sutton (Ed.), *Literary texts in an electronic age: Scholarly implications and library services* (Papers presented at the 1994 Clinic on Library Applications of Data Processing, April 10-12, 1994) (pp. 35-56). Urbana-Champaign: Graduate School of Library and Information Science, University of Illinois.

Technology Update: Digital Object Identifiers. (1998). *Online & CD-ROM Review, 22*(2), 115-118. See also: International DOI Foundation (1998). The Digital Object Identifier System [online]. Retrieved January 24, 2000 from the World Wide Web: http://www.doi.org/.

Tenopir, C., & Ro, J. S. (1990). *Full text databases.* New York: Greenwood Press.

Terry, D. (1991). Sidebar 4: Open Text Corporation. *Library Hi Tech, 9*(3), 7-44.

Weibel, S. (1994). The CORE Project: Technical shakedown phase and preliminary user studies. *OCLC Systems and Services, 10*(2 & 3), 99-102.

W3C: World Wide Web Consortium. (1999). *Resource Description Framework (RDF) Model and Syntax Specification: W3C Recommendation, 22 February 1999* [online]. Retrieved January 24, 2000 from the World Wide Web: http://www.w3.org/TR/1999/REC-rdf-syntax-19990222/.

W3C: World Wide Web Consortium. (1998). *Mathematical Markup Language (Math ML) 1.0 Specification: W3C Recommendation,07 April 1998* [online]. Retrieved January 24, 2000 from the World Wide Web: http://www.w3.org/TR/1998/REC-MathML-19980407/ [28 February 1999].

Federated Search of Scientific Literature

A Retrospective on the Illinois Digital Library Project

Bruce Schatz, William Mischo, Timothy Cole, Ann Bishop, Susan Harum, Eric Johnson, Laura Neumann, Hsinchun Chen, and Dorbin Ng

The NSF/DARPA/NASA Digital Libraries Initiative (DLI) project at the University of Illinois at Urbana-Champaign (UIUC), 1994-1998, had the goal of developing widely usable Web technology to effectively search technical documents on the Internet. Our efforts were concentrated on building an experimental testbed with tens of thousands of full-text journal articles from physics, engineering, and computer science, and making these articles available over the World Wide Web before they were available in print. The DLI testbed focused on using the document structure to provide federated searches across publisher collections. Our sociology research included the evaluation of its effectiveness under use by over 1,000 UIUC faculty and students, a user community an order of magnitude bigger than the last generation of research projects centered on searching scientific literature. Our technology research developed indexing of the contents of text documents to enable a federated search across multiple sources, testing this on millions of documents for semantic federation.

This article will discuss the achievements and difficulties we experienced over the past four years. In section 1 (the DLI testbed and Structured Documents), we will review our experiences in building the DLI testbed, in which repositories (indexed collections) of full-text multiple-source documents have been built and federated (merged and mapped), so that they appear as a single virtual collection. Section 2 (Testbed Evaluation and Sociology Research) presents the results of our user studies and evaluation of the testbed and its user community in addition to our work in investigating the social practices of digital libraries. We then describe, in section 3 (Semantic Indexing and Technology Research), our research to improve information retrieval technology through the development of the Interspace, which focuses on statistical technologies for semantic indexing that are scalable across subject domains. Section 4 (Multiple Views and Federated Search) describes our development of an Internet client for federated repositories, which allows the user to retrieve information from multiple servers by dynamically combining multiple indexes. Finally, in section 5 (Conclusion), we discuss our vision of the future of the Internet in the twenty-first century, where every community maintains its own repository of its own knowledge, and scalable semantics enables federation across repositories.

DLI TESTBED AND STRUCTURED DOCUMENTS

The overarching focus of the DLI testbed team has been on the design, development, and evaluation of mechanisms that provide effective access to full-text physics and engineering journal articles within an Internet environment. The primary goals of the testbed team were: (1) the construction and testing of a multi-publisher SGML-based full-text testbed employing flexible search and rendering capabilities and offering rich links to internal and external resources; (2) the integration of the testbed and other full-text repositories into the continuum of information resources offered to end-users within the library system; (3) determining the efficacy of full-text article searching vis-à-vis document surrogate searching, and exploring end-user full-text searching behavior in an attempt to identify user-searching needs; and (4) identifying models for effective publishing and retrieval of full-text articles within an Internet environment and employing these models in the testbed design and development.

Over the last four years, in conjunction with a number of professional societies, the testbed team has implemented a large-scale Web-based testbed of full-text journal articles featuring enhanced access and display capabilities. The Illinois DLI testbed is presently comprised of the article full-text in SGML format, the associated article metadata, and bit-mapped images of figures for sixty-three journal titles containing over 50,000 articles from five scholarly professional societies in physics and engineering. The full-text articles for the testbed have been contributed by the American Institute of Physics (AIP), the American Physical Society (APS), the American Society of Civil Engineers (ASCE), the Institute of Electrical and Electronics Engineers Computer Society (IEEE CS), and the Institution of Electrical Engineers (IEE).

The DLI testbed is based within the Grainger Engineering Library Information Center, a $22 million facility that opened in 1994 and is dedicated to the exploration of emerging information technologies. The Web-based retrieval system developed by the DLI testbed and evaluation teams is called DeLIver (Desktop Link to Virtual Engineering Resources). The DeLIver client, which replaced a Microsoft Windows-based custom client in use for the first two years of the project, has been in operation since

October 1997 and is being used by over 1,200 registered UIUC students and faculty and designated outside researchers. Detailed transaction log data of user search sessions (gathered and merged from database and Web servers) is being kept, and a preliminary analysis of user search patterns from 4,200 search sessions has been completed.

Figure 1 depicts a search session using the DLI Web client, DeLIver. The initial interface prompts the user that parts of the documents are searchable, and "plasma density" as a figure caption has been selected. The second interface displays the search results, showing four of the articles retrieved with "plasma density" in the figure caption. Note that the articles are from four different journals (federated repositories), and that "plasma density" is not found in the titles. The last interface displays an example of a figure retrieved in this manner. Note that SGML tags the complete structure of the document including figures and equations.

The cornerstones of the DLI testbed are the effective utilization of the article content and structure revealed by SGML and the production of the associated article-level metadata, which serves to normalize the heterogeneous SGML and provide short-entry display capability. The SGML is taken directly from the publisher's collections, then processed into a canonical format for federated search. The metadata also contain links to internal and external data, such as forward and backward links to other DLI testbed articles and links to A & I service databases and other repositories. The metadata and index files, which contain pointers to the full-text data, can be stored independently of, and separately from, the full text.

It is clear that a rich markup format such as XML (eXtensible Markup Language), which is a nearly complete instance of SGML, will become the language of open document systems. SGML permits documents to be treated as objects to be viewed, manipulated, and output. The major strength of SGML, in terms of its retrieval capabilities, lies in its ability to reveal the deep content and structure of a document. While SGML is becoming ubiquitous in the publishing world, it is still, for the most part, being generated by publishers as a byproduct rather than serving as an integral part of their production process.

The Document Type Definition (DTD) accompanying an individual publisher's SGML is the instrument that actually specifies the semantics and syntax of the tags to be used in the document markup. The DTD also specifies the rules that describe the manner in which the SGML tags may be applied to the documents. One of the major roadblocks in the successful deployment of the DLI testbed has been the processing involved with the heterogeneous DTDs directly from publishers. In the process of creating a viable DLI testbed, the Illinois testbed team developed a number of techniques to address problems and normalize SGML processing, indexing, storage, retrieval, and rendering.

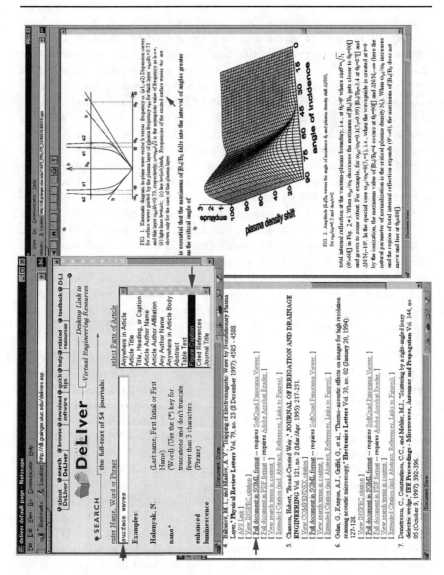

Figure 1. DLI Testbed Web-Based DeLIver Search Session

Another important concern of the DLI testbed group has been in exploring effective retrieval models for a Web-based electronic journal publishing system. It has become commonplace for both major and small-scale publishers to provide Internet (Web-based) access to their publications, including journal issues and articles. The DLI testbed team has proposed a distributed repository model which federates the individual publisher repositories of full-text documents. These distributed repositories are federated or connected by the extraction of normalized metadata and index data from the full-text which can then be searched via a parallel execution monitor. This model addresses the challenge of providing standardized and consistent subject, title, and author searching capabilities across these distributed and disparate repositories.

The DLI testbed team has succeeded in demonstrating the efficacy of the distributed repository model by producing cross-DTD metadata, providing parallel database querying and distributed retrieval techniques across a distinguished subset of the full-text repositories, and by establishing and employing an off-site repository at the site of an actual publisher (AIP).

In the four years of the grant, the testbed team has made significant progress in the development of a metadata specification to support standardized retrieval across repositories. This allowed for a short-entry display independent of the discrete full-text document repositories and links to associated testbed items, A & I service databases, and other repositories. SGML tag aliasing or normalization of the system was done to accommodate heterogeneous DTDs. Development was needed of the Web DeLIver and custom Windows clients for search, retrieval, and display across multiple discrete repositories to provide cross-repository retrieval from single-search command arguments.

Issues that came to the forefront during the project were connected with the rendering of SGML within the Softquad Panorama viewer and the rendering mathematics in particular. As a result of these difficulties, an international mathematics rendering conference was organized and held at the Grainger Library in May 1996.

Innovations by the testbed team include the integration of DeLIver with other retrieval services. An Ovid INSPEC and Compendex proxy with links to the DeLIver Testbed and other remote publisher repositories were implemented. Links from the bibliographies of retrieved DeLIver articles to other items contained in the testbed were incorporated as well as citation links from testbed articles that cite previous testbed articles. Links from the retrieved DeLIver articles and references in the bibliographies of retrieved DeLIver articles to INSPEC and Compendex database records in an Ovid system were also incorporated. DeLIver users may also re-execute the DeLIver search command arguments in the INSPEC/Compendex/CurrentContents periodical index databases.

This work has been accomplished with the cooperation and support of our publisher partners and through the use of commercial software from OpenText, Hewlett-Packard, SoftQuad, and Microsoft. The partnering relationship between the testbed team and its publishing partners was particularly strong, as evidenced by their assertion that the DLI was their "R&D" arm.

Technology transfer was fostered through frequent formal and informal meetings, quarterly newsletters updating research results, frequently updated Web pages, and an annual expense-paid workshop. DLI partners had access to DeLIver, the UIUC Web client, and hands-on consulting for SGML specifications. In addition, they received versions of the Windows custom client and processing code along with copies of research results, including statistics and user evaluation.

The strong partnering relationship is also evidenced by the agreement between the DLI and their partners to initiate a Collaborative Partners Program, which will provide for the continuation of the DLI testbed beyond the grant period. The Grainger Library is also a recipient of a three-year grant from DARPA to continue the SGML testbed.

The Collaborative Partners Program and the DARPA grant will allow the testbed team to continue researching issues connected with full-text article indexing, interface design, retrieval, and rendering. Continued contributions of materials from the publishing partners will allow for the increase of both the depth and breadth of the digital collection. Plans are also underway to extend testbed access to the Big 10 university consortium throughout the Midwest so as to enlarge the user population and further develop the distributed repository model.

TESTBED EVALUATION AND SOCIOLOGY RESEARCH

The DLI Social Science Team has pursued an integrated interdisciplinary research program that investigates the social practices of digital libraries (Bishop & Star, 1996). Throughout the course of the project, we have carried out user studies and evaluation work aimed at improving the DLI testbed. We are also working on documenting and analyzing extent and nature of testbed use, satisfaction, and impacts within the context of engineering work and communication. Both of these lines of work also inform our broader interests in contributing to existing knowledge about engineering work, use of scientific and engineering journals, and the changing information infrastructure.

We have pursued several specific research threads that are of particular relevance to understanding social practices associated with the development and use of federated online repositories of full-text documents. These include studies of the disaggregation of journal articles in the course of knowledge construction; how people make sense of new DLs they encounter; the convergence of communities of practice with information artifacts and infrastructure; and negotiating among multiple visions of a DL held by different stakeholders.

The DL Initiative has afforded us the opportunity to share ideas on human-centered design and evaluation with colleagues across the six projects, most notably those at Berkeley and Santa Barbara. We feel that our research has been greatly enriched by this association. Our experiences will be pooled in an edited monograph on research related to social aspects of digital library design and use planned for publication in 1999. The book aims to identify and discuss challenging issues that arise in socially-grounded approaches to studying digital libraries based on the recent work of leading researchers in the field. We feel the book will be of interest to digital library policy-makers, designers, implementers, and evaluators.

In conducting our research, we paid particular attention to the adaptation and application of traditional social science methods to studying social phenomena associated with information systems. We have employed a variety of qualitative and quantitative techniques for collecting and analyzing data. These include observation of engineering work and learning activities, interviews and focus groups with a range of potential and actual system users, usability testing, and large-scale user surveys. In addition, we have initiated a number of computer-mediated data-gathering techniques, such as user registration, exit polls displayed after an individual's DeLIver session, and system instrumentation (the creation of transaction logs). We are bringing the results of each of these methods together in order to triangulate our findings and provide a deeper understanding of the nature of digital library use and the social phenomena involved.

We currently have over 1,200 registered patrons of DeLIver representing University of Illinois faculty, students, and staff. About half of our users are graduate students, who also do the highest average number of searches. Approximately 75 percent of DeLIver patrons are men, mostly in the 23-29 age bracket. The relatively small number of faculty members who use the system seem to be intense users. There is a surprisingly wide audience for DeLIver, representing all campus engineering disciplines, science-related fields such as ecological modeling and biology, and other fields such as communications and psychology. We have found, however, that our heaviest users closely reflect the content of our testbed, which concentrates its holdings on journals from civil engineering, electrical and computer engineering, and computer science.

A preliminary analysis of recently completed user surveys ($N = 226$) suggests that people are generally satisfied with our system. The mean overall responses to three separate questions meant to gauge people's reaction to DeLIver was 3.5 (where one corresponded to "terrible," "frustrating," "inadequate search power" and five corresponded to "wonderful," "satisfying," and "adequate search power"). DeLIver transaction logs reveal the extent to which various system features have been used.

Analysis of over 4,200 sessions indicates that about 20 percent of sessions invoked the Extended Citation screen, while 38 percent of sessions resulted in viewing the full text of an article. In situated usability interviews, we found that the extent to which people use the available full text is compromised by the fact that they must download additional software in order to view it. Comments made by DeLIver users in interviews also suggest that new system features—like the Extended Citation screen—are bypassed, at least initially, in favor of familiar ways of handling print journal articles. While the Extended Citation screen allows users to identify and browse material in a manner that potential users said would be desirable, actual use requires an initial learning effort not demanded by following one's habitual manner of reading print material.

Given the nature of searching and display that is made possible through the use of SGML and the layered means of displaying search results, we have explored how researchers use journal components—such as abstracts, figures, equations, or bibliographic citations—in their work (Bishop, 1998). We have identified five basic purposes for use of article components: (1) to identify documents of interest; (2) to assess the relevance of an article before retrieving and reading the full text; (3) to create a customized document surrogate after retrieval that includes a combination of bibliographic and other elements—e.g., author's name, article title, tables; (4) to provide specific pieces of information such as an equation, a fact, or a diagram; and (5) to convey knowledge not easily rendered by words, especially through figures and tables.

Engineers describe a common pattern of utilizing document components to focus on and filter information in their initial reading of an article. They tend to read the title and abstract first and then skim section headings. Next, they look at lists, summary statements, definitions, and illustrations before focusing on key sections, reading conclusions, and skimming references. But engineers pursue unique practices after this initial reading as they disaggregate and reaggregate article components for use in their own work. Everyone takes scraps or reusable pieces of information from the article, but everyone does this differently—e.g., by using a marker to highlight text portions of interest or making a mental register of key ideas. People then create some kind of transitory compilation of reusable pieces, such as a personal bibliographic database, folders containing the first page of an article stapled to handwritten notes, or a pile of journal issues with key sections bookmarked. These intellectual and physical practices associated with component use seem to be based on a combination of tenure in the field, the nature of the task at hand, personal work habits, and cognitive style.

Our digital library also provides an opportunity to step back and take a broader look at the use of online digital collections and how people attempt to make sense of them. In analyzing results from several different data collection efforts, we have found that users can be confused by a newly encountered DL, and that it takes some time and interaction for them to decide what a particular system, like DeLIver, is. In usability tests, we identified patterns of user actions designed to uncover what sort of system our testbed was and what it could do. What first appeared to be a random trial and error use of the interface was actually structured exploration that occurred frequently across sessions.

We argue that users take a "cut and try approach" (Neumann & Ignacio, 1998) to help them differentiate our system from other genres of online systems, such as a general Web search engine or an online library catalog. In addition, users look for cues that indicate which conventions different platforms and interfaces hold. Because our DeLIver interface, in particular, draws on many different information system genres without carrying anyone's conventions through entirely, users are confused. For example, in one version of the system, all underlined terms did not represent hypertext links and, in the current version, not all the links are easily identifiable. Because there are no consistently followed conventions for interfaces to Web-based digital libraries, we need to find a way to signal to users what is and is not different about the individual systems they encounter.

Finally, one other area of general research deals with the larger implications of our changing information infrastructure. Communities of practice converge with information artifacts and information infrastructure to produce the "ready-to-hand-ness" of particular resources. Transparency is created and maintained through access to, and participation in, communities of practice and their associated information worlds. We have investigated this through three case studies: (1) of academic researchers, (2) of a profession creating a classification of work practices, and (3) of a large-scale classification system (Star, Bowker, & Neumann, 1998).

There have been many hurdles that we have overcome and challenges in our work that we are still dealing with. Many of these stem from the difficulties of resolving the multiple facets of this large and distributed project. All the different teams on the project bring different expertise, interests, and assumptions about how everything should work. We have often found ourselves at the crux of these differences in our roles of eliciting user feedback, running usability tests, meeting with reference librarians charged with incorporating our DLI testbed into existing library services, and taking broader theoretical perspectives. Negotiating these multiple and sometimes competing visions was the subject of one study in which we focused on understanding the ways in which potential use, new and old infrastructure, and large project organization interact.

Just as our social science research can be different things to different people, so can our digital library. DeLIver is a hybrid system, something of a research system, a system to demonstrate to various stakeholder groups, and also a production system upon whose stability users rely. This mix was particularly apparent during DeLIver's roll-out in October 1997. Our team, in conjunction with the Testbed Team, struggled to make sense of, and deal with, initial user access barriers in the form of authentication and registration procedures. Situating (potential) use in the real world forced us to think about who our most likely audience was, what they were probably most interested in using our system for, and how best to reach them.

SEMANTIC INDEXING AND TECHNOLOGY RESEARCH

Improving World Wide Web searching beyond full-text retrieval requires using document structure in the short-term and document semantics in the long-term. As the testbed team made progress in research with SGML, our Technology Research team focused on the development of the Interspace. The Interspace is a vision of the future Internet where each community maintains its own repository of its own knowledge (Schatz, 1997). For amateur classifiers to be comparable to today's professionals, information infrastructure must provide substantial support for semantic indexing and semantic retrieval.

The focus of the Interspace is on scalable technologies for semantic indexing that work generically across all subject domains (Schatz, Johnson, Cochrane, & Chen, 1996). Analogues of concepts and categories are automatically generated. Concept spaces can be used to boost a search by interactively suggesting alternative terms (Chen, Yim, Fye, & Schatz, 1995; Schatz, Johnson, Cochrane, & Chen, 1996). Category maps can be used to boost navigation by interactively browsing clusters of related documents (Chen, Yim, Fye, & Schatz, 1998). Collectively we refer to these techniques as semantic indexing.

The scalable semantics algorithms rely on statistical techniques, which correlate the context of phrases within the documents. Over the past several years using DLI materials, we have used NCSA supercomputers to compute progressively larger collections until the scale of entire disciplines, such as engineering, has been reached. We use supercomputers as time machines to simulate the world of a billion repositories by partitioning a large existing collection into discipline subcollections, which are the equivalent of community repositories.

Concept spaces were generated in 1995 for 400K abstracts from INSPEC (electrical engineering and computer science) and in 1996 for 4M abstracts from Compendex (all of engineering, some thirty-eight broad subjects). The first computation took one day of supercomputer time (Chen, Schatz, Ng, Martinez, Kirchoff, & Lin, 1996) and the second took ten days of high-end time on the HP Convex Exemplar (Schatz, 1997). The second computation provided a comprehensive simulation of community repositories for 1,000 collections across all of engineering, generated by partitioning the abstracts along the subject classification hierarchy.

Concept spaces are collections of abstract concepts that are generated from concrete objects. Traditionally, the objects have been text documents and the concepts all canonical noun phrases. The concept spaces are then the co-occurrence frequencies between related terms with the documents of the collection.

Figure 2 depicts an example of the use of concept spaces for engineering literature (Chen, Martinez, Kirchoff, Ng, & Schatz, 1998). The upper window displays abstract indexes for categories and concepts, while the lower window displays concrete indexes for document collections. The pane in the upper left of the figure shows an integrated list of abstract indexes over the INSPEC, Compendex, and Patterns collections. INSPEC and Compendex are standard commercial bibliographic databases, and Patterns is a Software Engineering community repository.

The upper left-hand pane is a snapshot of a query session in Software Engineering incorporating all three indexes: Computers and Data Processing from the Compendex index, Software engineering techniques from the INSPEC index, and Design Patterns from the Patterns index. The two panes to the right of the upper window show portions of an automatically generated concept space for the INSPEC categories "Software Engineering Techniques" and "Object Oriented Programming." The concept space allows the user to interactively refine a search by selecting concepts that have been automatically generated and presented to the user. In the example below, the user has specified "complex object" and the system returned a list of related concepts such as "configuration management."

If the concept space is further navigated (not shown), additional related concepts, such as "revision control system," can be found. Such concepts may be used in conducting a full-text search as portrayed in the "Full Text Search" pane below the concept space display. This allows the user to descend to the level of actual objects in a collection at any time. In the lower left pane, the user has performed a full-text search on the concept space term "revision control system" and the system has identified several abstracts containing this term with the one selected by the user displayed in the lower right pane.

The Interspace consists of multiple spaces at the category, the concept, and the object levels. Within the course of an interaction session, a user will move across different spaces at different levels of abstraction and across different subject domains. For example, the system enables users to locate desired terms in the concept space by starting from broad terms then traversing into narrow terms specific to that document collection.

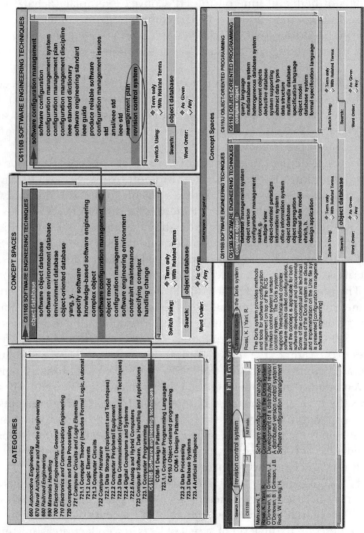

Figure 2. Semantic Indexing for Engineering Community Repositories

They can then move into document space to perform a full-text search by dragging the concept term into the document space search window. This sequence is shown for "revision control system."

Finally, to search a subject domain they are less familiar with, users can begin within the concept space for a familiar subject domain, then choose another concept space for the unfamiliar domain and navigate across spaces based on common terms. This has been depicted as follows: first, the user has identified "complex object" as a desirable search term and refined the search by locating the related term "revision control system." Next, the user has determined to pursue the object-oriented theme in greater detail and wishes to switch from the "Software Engineering Techniques" subject domain into the "Object Oriented Programming" domain.

The result of this concept switching is depicted in Figure 2, where the portion of the corresponding concept space for "Object Oriented Programming" has been displayed in the upper right pane. The user can now deepen the search by browsing related terms of "complex object" in the "Object Oriented Programming" subject domain. Such a fluid flow across levels and subjects supports semantic interoperability and is our approach toward vocabulary switching (Chen, Martinez, Ng, & Schatz, 1997). This form of interactive concept switching by space navigation is a key reason for naming the system the Interspace.

MULTIPLE VIEWS AND FEDERATED SEARCH

Complete search sessions across multiple sources are necessary to handle effectively scientific literature. The DLI testbed efforts provided support for federated search across the document structures from different publisher repositories. The user could then use a single high-level structure, such as author or caption, and have it automatically translated into the appropriate SGML tags for each document. The research efforts provided support for federated search across the document contents from different publisher repositories. Higher-level indexes for term suggestion were automatically generated; these enabled the user to provide a general term and choose, from a list of suggestions, a specific term actually useful for a search.

These results make it clear that general network information retrieval systems must integrate multiple views. Traditional information retrieval has supported only a single view—i.e., it sends a query to an index and returns a result. This is the model currently supported within the commercial online systems and within the World Wide Web. A multiple view interface supports complete sessions with a federated search of multiple indexes and with dynamic combination across the results of different searches.

We have developed a multiple-view, multiple-source information retrieval client and tested it on a prototype basis with the sources available within our DLI project. IODyne is custom software that runs on the PC Windows 95/NT platform (Schatz, Johnson, Cochrane, & Chen, 1996). The prototype can retrieve records from various kinds of text sources (SQL, Z39.50, Opentext) and provides search term suggestion from specially prepared subject thesauri and concept spaces. The user can simultaneously display and compare results from multiple bibliographic sources, as well as multiple suggestion sources, and can drag and drop objects from any

window into any other window to create new queries and present different views of data.

Figure 3 illustrates a multiple view session with indexes and protocols
from the DLI project. For text search, the testbed SGML repository is
accessed via the Opentext search engine and the INSPEC bibliographic
database via the Ovid Z39.50 proxy. For term suggestion, the INSPEC thesaurus is handled within a built-in IODyne browser, and the concept spaces
for INSPEC come from the Research semantic index computations.

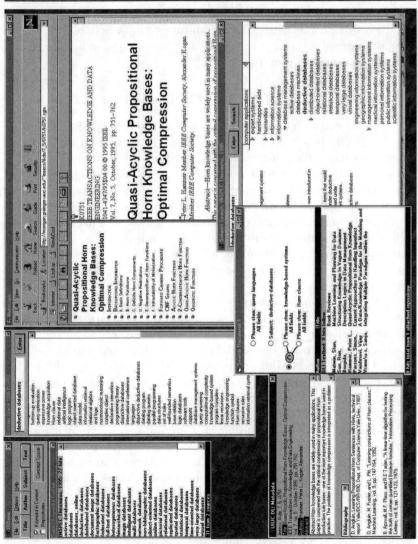

Figure 3. Multiple View Interface for Term Suggestion and Full-Text Search

In a typical session, a person would use the term suggestion sources to identify relevant terms and then the text search sources in order to retrieve relevant documents. The window at lower center is a search document with an SGML engineering repository attached to it. It contains several queries including a Boolean query. The Boolean query is selected, displaying its results in the lower half of the search document. The bibliographic record for one of the retrieved articles is at the lower left, and the full SGML document is displayed in the Netscape browser window at right, behind the search document and INSPEC thesaurus display.

The thesaurus display navigates subject hierarchies in thesaurus and classification systems. To perform a bibliographic search with any subject identifier in the thesaurus display, you drag it and drop it into the search document. Here "deductive databases" were used for a search. Often, the human-indexer subject thesaurus terms are too general for effective search directly but are used to navigate the machine-indexer concept spaces which contain all of the collection terms.

The concept space display, at top center, serves this detailed term suggestion. Search terms listed in it can be dropped onto the search document to perform bibliographic searches; the two terms in the Boolean search, "knowledge-based systems" and "Horn clause," were obtained from the concept space after dragging in "deductive databases" from the thesaurus. The Keyword in Context window, along the upper lefthand edge, shows terms matching a typed entry.

CONCLUSION

Both the DLI testbed and the research efforts of the UIUC DLI project achieved major success. The testbed efforts built a production system with federated search across structured documents. The articles arrive in a production stream directly from major scientific publishers in full-text SGML and are fully federated at the DTD level with a Web interface. The testbed collection is currently the largest existing federated repository of SGML articles from scientific literature. The DLI testbed users represent a population an order of magnitude bigger than the last generation research system for search of scientific literature. The testbed evaluation performed comprehensive methodologies at both a fine-grain level with user interviews and a large-scale level with transaction logs. Such results will lead shortly to practical commercial technologies for federating structured documents across the Internet.

The research efforts built an experimental system with semantic indexes from document content. Concept spaces are generated for term suggestion and integrated with text search via a multiple view interface. The research computations are the largest ever in information science.

They represent the first time that semantic indexes using generic technology have been generated on collections with millions of documents. They are the first large-scale step toward scalable semantics and statistical indexes with domain-independent computations.

The Internet of the twenty-first century will radically transform the interaction with knowledge. Traditionally, online information has been dominated by data centers with large collections indexed by trained professionals. The rise of the World Wide Web and the information infrastructure of distributed personal computing have rapidly developed the technologies of collections for independent communities. In the future, online information will be dominated by small collections maintained and indexed by the community members themselves.

The information infrastructure must similarly be radically different to support indexing of community collections and searching across such small collections. The base infrastructure will be knowledge networks rather than transmission networks. Users will consider themselves to be navigating in the Interspace, across logical spaces of semantic indexes, rather than in the Internet, across physical networks of computer servers.

Future knowledge networks will rely on scalable semantics, on automatically indexing small collections so that they can effectively be searched within the Interspace of a billion repositories. The most important feature of the infrastructure is therefore support of correlation across the indexed collections. Just as the transmission networks of the Internet are connected via switching machines that switch packets, the knowledge networks of the Interspace will be connected via switching machines that switch concepts.

ACKNOWLEDGMENTS

This work was supported by the National Science Foundation (NSF), the Defense Advanced Research Projects Agency (DARPA), and the National Aeronautics and Space Administration (NASA) under Cooperative Agreement No. IRI-94-11318COOP. We thank the American Institute of Physics (AIP), the American Physical Society (APS), the American Society of Civil Engineers (ASCE), the Institute of Electrical and Electronics Engineers Computer Society (IEEE CS), and the Institution of Electrical Engineers (IEE) for making their SGML materials available to us on an experimental basis. Engineering Index (EI) and IEE kindly provided Compendex and INSPEC respectively.

Many people have contributed to the research discussed here. In particular, we thank Robert Wedgeworth, Kevin Powell, Ben Gross, William Pottenger, Donal O'Connor, Robert Ferrer, Tom Habing, Hanwen Hsiao, Emily Ignacio, Cecelia Merkel, Bob Sandusky, Eric Larson, S. Leigh Star,

Andrea Houston, Pauline Cochrane, Larry Jackson, Mike Folk, Kevin Gamiel, Joseph Futrelle, William Wendling, Roy Campbell, Robert McGrath, Duncan Lawrie, and Leigh Estabrook.

REFERENCES

Bishop, A., & Star, S. L. (1996). Social informatics for digital library use and infrastructure. In M. E. Williams (Ed.), *Annual review of information science and technology* (vol. 31, pp. 301-401). Medford, NJ: Information Today.

Bishop, A. (1998). Digital libraries and knowledge disaggregation: The use of journal article components. In I. H. Witten, R. M. Akscyn & F. M. Shipman (Eds.), *Digital libraries '98* (The third ACM International Conference Digital Libraries, June). New York: Association for Computing Machinery.

Chen, H.; Yim, T.; Fye, D.; & Schatz, B. (1995). Automatic thesaurus construction for an electronic community system. *Journal of the American Society for Information Science, 46*(3), 175-193.

Chen, H.; Schatz, B.; Ng, T. D.; Martinez, J.; Kirchhoff, A.; & Lin, C. (1996). A parallel computing approach to creating engineering concept spaces for semantic retrieval: The Illinois digital library project. *IEEE Transaction Pattern Analysis and Machine Intelligence, 18*(8), 771-782.

Chen, H.; Martinez, J.; Ng, T. D.; & Schatz, B. (1997). A concept space approach to addressing the vocabulary problem in scientific information retrieval: An experiment on the Worm Community System. *Journal of the American Society for Information Science, 48* (1), 17-31.

Chen, H.; Houston, A.; Sewell, R.; & Schatz, B. (1998). Internet browsing and searching: User evaluations of category map and concept space techniques. *Journal of the American Society for Information Science, 49*(7), 582-603.

Chen, H.; Martinez, J.; Kirchhoff, A.; Ng, T. D.; & Schatz, B. (1998). Alleviating search uncertainty through concept associations: Automatic indexing, co-occurrence analysis, and parallel computing. *Journal of the American Society for Information Science, 49*(3), 206-216.

Neumann, L., & Ignacio, E. (1998). Trial and error as a learning strategy in system use. In C. M. Preston (Ed.), *ASIS '98* (Proceedings of the 61st American Society Information Science Annual Meeting, Pittsburgh, PA, October). Medford, NJ: Information Today.

Schatz, B.; Johnson, E.; Cochrane, P.; & Chen, H. (1996). Interactive term suggestion for users of digital libraries: Using subject thesauri and co-occurrence lists for information retrieval. In E. A. Fox & G. Marchionini (Eds.), *Proceedings of the first ACM International Conference Digital Libraries* (Bethesda, MD, March) (pp 126-133). New York: Association for Computing Machinery.

Schatz, B.; Mischo, W.; Cole, T.; Hardin, J.; Bishop, A.; & Chen, H. (1996). Federating diverse collections of scientific literature. *Computer, 29*(5), 28-36.

Schatz, B. (1997). Information retrieval in digital libraries: Bringing search to the Net. *Science, 275*(January), 327-334.

Star, S. L.; Bowker, G.; & Neumann, L. (1998). *Transparency beyond the individual level of scale: Convergence between information artifacts and communities of practice.* Unpublished manuscript.

FROM USABILITY TO USE
MEASURING SUCCESS OF TESTBEDS IN THE REAL WORLD

Laura J. Neumann and Ann Peterson Bishop[1]

INTRODUCTION

In 1994, as part of its commitment to the National Information Infrastructure (NII), the NSF, DARPA, and NASA funded six digital library projects at different universities (under the Digital Libraries Initiative—called "DLI" for short). Our Illinois DLI is a distributed multi-disciplinary project. Computer scientists, librarians, and social scientists worked together to develop an SGML database and protocols for federating repositories of data. The testbed team has constructed a prototype system that contains the full text of over fifty engineering, physics, and computer science journals. Some of the innovative aspects of our DLI project can be seen in DeLIver, the Web-based search interface to the testbed.[2] Through SGML markup of the scientific articles and enhanced search features, users can search for, and display, information from individual parts—e.g., "MIT" in author affiliation or "spectrum" in a figure caption. Users can also display the full text of the article at their desktops via the Web.

Our Social Science Team was charged with carrying out user studies and evaluation work on the project—a broad charter. All the different teams on the project bring different expertise, interests, and assumptions about how the DLI project should work and what it is about. We have often found ourselves at the crux of these differences in our multiple roles of providing user feedback, running usability tests, meeting with the reference librarians who are responsible for incorporating the system into the library, testing new methods of study, and taking broader theoretical perspectives. Over the last four years, as our work has grown out of moving between these different expectations, we have had to understand these multiple, and sometimes competing, visions and decide what the project is about, who its target audience is, and how best to reach and serve that audience (Neumann & Star, 1996).

At the same time that our work is many things to many different people, so is our DLI testbed itself. DeLIver is a hybrid system: something of a research system, a system to demonstrate to the project sponsors, and a system in production mode that users rely on (Bishop, 1998a). Each of these facets of the system implies different strategies and foci of research for the Social Science Team. We have approached dealing with this by tacking between the "usability" and "use" issues. It is really only in the last year, when our system began to have a substantial body of users, that use and usability began to merge. Before that, our work was devoted to needs assessment and the study of the phenomena and behavior that comprise science and engineering work practices, including the creation, exchange, and search for information.

HISTORY OF THE SOCIAL SCIENCE TEAM

The DLI Social Science Team is comprised of researchers with expertise ranging from qualitative research to computer programming to collecting transaction logs. We perform both formative and summative evaluations aimed at improving system design and documenting system use. At the same time that we are gaining new knowledge about the use of our system, we are trying new methods for studying the use of our digital library. Both of these lines of work also inform our broader interests in learning about the work habits of our potential and actual users, use of scientific and engineering journals, and use of digital libraries generally. To these ends, we have conducted needs assessments studies and have provided ongoing user feedback to system designers. We are working on documenting and analyzing extent and nature of testbed use, satisfaction, and impacts in the context of broader issues surrounding the changing information infrastructure. We have had to develop new methods for capturing user behavior that spans the online and offline environments, and we have made an attempt to assess these methods and discuss them with our scholarly community (Bishop, 1995, 1996; Bishop & Star, 1996). In this discussion, we will present an overview of our findings on usability and use as well as a summary of some of the lessons we have learned in the course of our research.[3]

METHODS

Our goal is to create an integrated research program, combining broad studies of use with deep studies of social phenomena connected to the use of our digital library. We have done this through a wide variety of both qualitative and quantitative methods, such as observation of engineering work and learning activities, interviews and focus groups with a range of potential and actual system users, usability testing (particularly following Monk, Wright, Haber, and Davenport, 1993), and large-scale user surveys. In addition, we are employing a number of automated data gathering techniques, such as user registration, online feedback, and system instrumentation (the creation of testbed transaction logs).

We have also been experimenting with methods such as online "exit polls"—a short survey that pops up during a session after a particular amount of time has elapsed. We adapted our instrument from one created by researchers at the Alexandria DLI project in Santa Barbara. These polls ask about the purpose of the session as well as the user's success in accomplishing this purpose and include a few other questions about users' overall impressions of DeLIver. A second method that we have found to be fruitful is one we call "situated usability" interviews. These involve selecting people who fit particular criteria from the pool of registered system users and pulling their transaction logs. Using screen dumps of the different parts of the system and the transaction logs as conversation prompts, we asked the targeted individuals about things that they had done with the system, why they had done them, and any comments they had about usability issues. We are bringing the results of each of these methods together in order to triangulate the findings and provide a deeper understanding of the nature of digital library use and the social phenomena involved.

USABILITY TO USE

Up until this past year of work, our research efforts felt largely fragmented. On the one hand, we were doing usability tests to aid in interface development and we were talking with users who were testing earlier versions of the system. On the other hand, we were doing mini-ethnographies examining information gathering in "real world" settings. The one set of activities did not much overlap with the other. However, when our DeLIver's "roll-out" began in October 1997, pieces from the full range of our data collection initiatives began to fall into place to form a more coherent picture of use (see Bishop, 1998a for a more extensive discussion of what follows). In being forced into thinking about how we should gauge success and how we should measure use, we were able to find a way to bring together all of the work we had done up to that point.

MAKING THAT TRANSITION: ROLL-OUT PANIC

To access DeLIver, prospective users must first enter their University of Illinois network identification number in an online "NetID form." This allows the publishers of material in the testbed a reasonable assurance that access is restricted to campus affiliates in accordance with our original agreement. After filling in their NetID, prospective users must complete a registration form that provides basic demographic data that will help us learn more about who is using DeLIver.

Analysis of the Web logs revealed that, between November 1 to 14, 1997, 1,276 (83 percent) of 1,540 attempted accesses were abandoned at the NetID form. Of the 186 people who entered a NetID, 91 (49 percent) stopped at the registration form. Obviously, these grim numbers lead to a certain amount of panic on the project, so the Social Science and Testbed Development teams met to discuss the dilemma. The debates centered on both why we should reduce barriers to use and how to do so. In answering the "why" question, the hybrid nature of our project was made clear: in terms of creating a production system, some people were primarily concerned with making the system easier to access; in terms of demonstrating our system to key stakeholders, others were concerned with showing high usage statistics; and as a research project, we all wanted to draw users in so that we could learn more about digital libraries and their use.

Discussion of what could be done to reduce barriers to use included simplifying the testbed functionality by removing the multiple search options, removing the login and registration procedures entirely for awhile, streamlining the login and registration forms, and finally, stepping up publicity by pinpointing the hubs of use. The last two options were selected as the least detrimental to project goals and were given a try.

In addition, this situation caused us to reflect on what the "bail outs" were telling us. We turned to our own and others' more general research on digital library and Web use to reframe our thinking. A number of issues were revealed:

- People aren't UIUC affiliates. We had to think of the potential pool of people who had access to our login screen as anyone on the Web. Obviously, the vast majority of Web users do not attend, or work with or for, our university. These people would turn away when asked for a "UIUC NetID."
- Lack of awareness among the target audience. In reflecting on research that we and others had done, we knew that our system was most likely to be useful to graduate students in a particular set of fields (Star, Bowker, & Neumann, forthcoming). Up to this point, general publicity was primarily in libraries—and people in our target disciplines are not heavy library users (Entlich et al., 1997; Lancaster, 1995; Pinelli, 1991; Garvey & Griffith, 1980; and others).
- Registration form equals fee. Given the variety of systems available on the Web in conjunction with some services available at our university, potential users had reason to suspect that they were being asked to register so that they could be billed for their system use.

- Lack of real need—just surfing. The DLI project has gained a certain amount of visibility among people interested in building digital libraries. It was possible that these people, and others, were simply curious about our site and surfed by to take a look. When presented with the NetID form, they left.
- Confusion—"NetID? What do I do now?" Use of a NetID for course registration and other purposes is fairly new to our university. It was entirely possible that people did not know what a NetID was.
- Registration form is too long. Our initial registration form was longer than a single average screen length. When confronted with what appeared to be an endless list of questions, it is possible that potential users did not think that using the system was worth the time needed to complete the required registration form.

The question of how we should measure use and define success also became salient at this point. What could we expect as a reasonable number of users? In addition, the question of what *was* a "real use" of the system was raised. In terms of success, we looked at the real numbers of our pool of "potential users." There are approximately 1,900 graduate students and 400 faculty members in various engineering areas, physics, and computer science at this university. The scale of users should be in this ballpark. The limited collection in our testbed does not comprehensively cover any of these areas, and some types of engineering are not represented at all.

When considering the likely frequency of use, we had to consider which of these people would actually be interested in our journals and, of those interested, which potential users would not have their own paper subscription that they would prefer to use? In addition, our research indicated that our users' searching and browsing habits followed cycles of research and of the semester—when would they be likely users? The time frames that were examined are just before finals at the University of Illinois and during the winter break. Students are studying for finals or writing up projects; faculty are grading and doing catch-up work. Heavy use of our system was not likely at this time (Ignacio, Neumann, & Sandusky, 1995). Finally, our expectations of use should be modified by the amount of time needed to effectively market the system, allow new users to learn the system, and allow people to develop into committed users.

A useful strategy to frame usage statistics will be to gather comparative data. The number of people who use the university's other online library systems, how often the paper journals are used, and the number of registered users for other digital library systems—including an earlier version of our own—must all be considered.

Ultimately, after the "NetID" form was clarified and better explained to users, after it was made clear that the system was free and the registration form was abbreviated, the "bailout" statistics improved some-what (see Table 1).

TABLE 1.
"BAILOUT" STATISTICS FOR THE DeLIVER SYSTEM

Dates	No. attempted accesses/ No. stopped	No. people who entered NetID/ No. people stopped
Nov. 1- 14, 1997	1540/ 1276 (83 percent)	186/ 91 (49 percent)
Dec. 9- 19	462/ 259 (56 percent)	113/ 35 (31 percent)
Jan. 1- 23, 1998	560/ 240 (43 percent)	182/ 49 (27 percent)
Feb. 18- Apr. 9	1978/750 (38 percent)	571/162 (29 percent)

The definition of "real use" of the system is a topic still under consideration. Our project, and DeLIver in particular, has gained some visibility on campus. It was brought to our attention that several large classes that deal with interface design have used DeLIver as a case study to be critiqued by the students and discussed in class. No doubt many of the undergraduates from non-science related disciplines accessed the system for this reason. DeLIver is also used as an example system in information retrieval classes in the library school. Many librarians in the science-related libraries have logged into the system so that they are somewhat familiar with it in case a patron at the library should ask a question about it. An untold number of people also log onto the system just to "check it out" or "mess around" to see what it is for. It is an open question whether or not these people should be considered "real" users. They are not interacting with the content of the system or the interface in order to complete work tasks by accessing information in the scientific and technical journals. However, who are we to say what people "should" do with our system? On the other hand, if the goal is to discuss what researchers find valuable about DeLIver, or to see if the ability to search parts of the article has proved useful in retrieving relevant items, then the logs of people who used this part of the system "just to try it" or to critique the interface could be misleading.

Working with some of the nitty-gritty aspects of our registration and transaction logging data has led us to think more deeply about broader theoretical questions. As we have noted, our definition of use depends on the identity and intentions of our user, as well as on how he or she perceives and interacts with DLs and information more generally. Our findings begin to address these larger questions.

UNDERSTANDING DIGITAL LIBRARY USE

Several data collection and analysis efforts are still underway, such as transaction logging and large-scale survey analysis, but we have gathered some preliminary information on the extent and nature of use that will be addressed more comprehensively later. In addition, we have investigated other areas related to social practices and digital libraries. These are sketched out below.

WHO ARE OUR USERS? WHAT ARE THEY DOING?

From our registration process, we know that as of 5 June 1998, we have 1,174 registered patrons of DeLIver. "Patron" refers to someone who is neither working for the project nor employed at the library where our project is based. Approximately 75 percent of our patrons are men, 70 percent speak English as their primary language, and they are mainly in the 23-29 age bracket. About 50 percent of DeLIver users are graduate students, and 30 percent are undergraduates. There is a surprisingly wide audience for the system. All kinds of engineering and other science-related fields such as ecological modeling, materials sciences, and biology—as well as users from fields such as communications, education, and psychology—are represented among DeLIver users' primary field of study.

We have found that, in spite of this wide audience, our heaviest users (naturally) closely reflect the content of our testbed, which holds a large collection of items from civil engineering, electrical and computer engineering, and computer science. People who identify their primary field as "engineering—general" also represent a large percentage of our user population and have the highest average number of sessions. The graduate students login most often (compared to faculty and undergrads) but not by much. The relatively small number of faculty members who use the system seem to be intense users. A preliminary look at over 200 recently completed user surveys shows that respondents are generally satisfied with our system and its search power.

When we begin to delve into use of the system, our transaction logs will provide the most information. At this time, we are still working with those data, and results are not yet available. However, interviews, usability tests, and logs from a previous version of the system indicate that people are using multiple search terms, but that they are not taking advantage of searching different parts of the articles. In interviews, on the other hand, people say that this type of search is a nice idea.

Interviews reveal that users often take advantage of the ability to see the abstract of the articles either instead of, or before, retrieving the full text. Although several people we talked to were looking for components of articles, they strongly stated that they are not interested in seeing "only" the figures or equations because without the surrounding text, these could not be evaluated. We have found that the extent to which people use the available full text is complicated by the fact that extra software is necessary to access it. When the software is available and functioning properly, the full text is used—however, downloading the software onto a local machine and getting it to work is no simple task. Accessing the full text also requires either a Windows environment and the use of Netscape or that a PDF version of the desired article be available and the user's machine have a PDF viewer (not all publishers have made a PDF version of their articles available—at last count it was about two-thirds of the contents of the database). A few of the users did not understand the difference between SGML and PDF, and others did not understand the configuration of software needed. We have already talked to several users who have had many problems with the technical aspects of viewing articles in DeLIver.

COMPONENT USE

Given the nature of searching and display that is made possible through the use of SGML and the layered means of displaying search results, we have explored how researchers use journal components—such as abstracts, figures, equations, or bibliographic citations—in their work (Bishop, 1998b). We have identified five basic purposes for use of article components: (1) to identify documents of interest; (2) to assess the relevance of an article before retrieving and reading the full text; (3) to create a customized document surrogate after retrieval that includes a combination of bibliographic and other elements (e.g., author's name, article title, tables); (4) to provide specific pieces of information such as an equation, a fact, or a diagram; and (5) to convey knowledge not easily rendered by words, especially through figures and tables.

Engineers in our study describe a common pattern of utilizing document components to zoom in on and to filter information in their initial reading of an article. They tend to read the title and abstract first and then skim section headings. Next, they look at lists, summary statements, definitions, and illustrations before focusing on key sections, reading conclusions, and skimming references. But engineers pursue unique practices after this initial reading as they disaggregate and reaggregate article components for use in their own work. Everyone takes scraps or reusable pieces of information from the article, but everyone does this differently—for example, by using a marker to highlight text portions of interest or making a mental register of key ideas. People then create some kind of transitory compilation of reusable pieces such as a personal bibliographic database, folders containing the first page of an article stapled to handwritten notes, or a pile of journal issues with key sections bookmarked. These intellectual and physical practices associated with component use seem to be based on a combination of tenure in the field, the nature of the task at hand, personal work habits, and cognitive style.

MAKING SENSE OF NEW ONLINE SYSTEMS

Our digital library also provides an opportunity to step back and take a broader look at the use of online digital collections and how people attempt to make sense of them. By analyzing data from several different data collection efforts, we have found that users can be confused by a system like ours, and it takes some time and interaction for them to discern what the system is. In many usability tests, we identified patterns of user actions designed to "uncover" what sort of system they were using and what it could do. What first appeared to be a random "trial and error" use of the interface was actually structured exploration that occurred frequently across sessions. We argue that users take a "cut and try" approach to differentiate our system from other genres of online systems such as a general Web search engine or an online public access library catalog. In addition, users were looking for cues that would tell them which conventions of different platforms and different interfaces would hold in DeLIver's environment. Because our DeLIver interface draws on many different genres without carrying any one through entirely, users are confused—for example, in one version of the system, all underlined terms were not linked and, in the current version, not all the links are easily identifiable. However, there are no defined conventions for interfaces to Web-based digital libraries, and we need to find a way to signal to users what is and is not different about the digital library systems they encounter (Neumann & Ignacio, 1998).

INFORMATION CONVERGENCE

One other area of general research deals with the larger implications of our changing information infrastructure. Star, Bowker, and Neumann (forthcoming) discuss how communities of practice converge with information artifacts and information infrastructure to produce the "ready-to-hand-ness" of particular resources. This coming together of infrastructure, community-based work practices, and bits of information is what appears to be transparency. This is created and maintained through access to, and participation in, communities of practice and their associated information worlds. This is described more fully through three case studies of academic researchers, of a profession creating a classification of work practices, and of a large-scale classification system.

In the case of academic researchers, as a person becomes a full member of a community, he or she has an ease of access to information that is a part of day-to-day living and work. These processes are mostly invisible to outsiders and are generally not made up of formal information systems, but rather colleague networks, professional duties, and personal collections. What appears from the outside as transparent access to a field of information is really a product of the particular social location of the individual. Professions and communities also deliberately create convergence on language and practice in order to demonstrate a unified whole. Across levels of scale, "transparency and ease of use for groups are products of a shifting alignment of information resources and social practices" (Star, Bowker, & Neumann, forthcoming). Work on digital libraries can be informed by this research in that it makes an implicit level of information-gathering explicit and gives a clearer definition of the role of formalized systems.

LESSONS LEARNED

The most important lesson that we have learned in our work is that triangulation of data on all aspects of use and usability is crucial. It is this process that has allowed us to pursue the different social issues surrounding DL use as well as dealing with specific usability issues of our DLI search system. Triangulation involves planning and work to build on past data collection efforts and methods in order to complete a holistic picture of use. A full understanding of use becomes much more attainable when complementary evidence is merged from multiple sources.

A second lesson involves defining the place of user support and marketing of the system. This involves such things as answering user questions about the system, writing documentation for "help" pages, and distributing pamphlets and putting up signs about the system. Our project did not explicitly assign the responsibility for these tasks to particular project members, and some things have slipped through the cracks only to have people scramble to deal with them later.

In terms of some of our data collection efforts, we are now more aware of the realities of online data collection. Asking users to register in order to gather general information about them has a trade-off: while some users will not use the system because of it, analytical power is gained by requiring some basic information. Surveys administered only online will have an extremely low return rate. This is not unusual. Others have reported similar experiences (Entlich et al., 1997; Borghuis et al., 1996). There have been few people, as far as we can tell, who have "faked" information or supplied dummy information. What has been more frequent is users declining to answer. Fully 25 percent decline to answer our ethnicity question, 10 percent decline age, but only 1 percent decline gender.

The transaction log data have been particularly challenging to work with. Because DeLIver is Web based, there are some aspects of system instrumentation that are more difficult than when dealing with stand alone systems. Data are gathered in a continuous stream—although sometimes the system retrieves results or the full text in several chunks, and parsing individual actions has proven difficult. Decisions had to be made about how to define a session in terms of time elapsed without a subsequent user action. Finally, using default settings on the search form has been problematic—it becomes impossible to differentiate between people who actually wanted to search, for example, the full text as opposed to those people who did not notice that there was an option to search only a certain part of the article.

Using the Web for surveying users has taught us to expect extremely low response rates. However, the convenience of using a Web survey as opposed to a mass mailing means that sometimes this is an attractive option. Finally, as we have already noted, we have used several different styles of surveys on the Web: feedback forms, pop-up exit polls, and finally, a large-scale user survey that was both sent out on paper and was made available on the Web. It will be difficult to compare responses due to the widely varying response rates between them.

CONCLUSION

Usability and use are two sides of the same coin. Three years of moving between the two types of study has involved a series of managerial and time allocation challenges but, as the project nears an end, it is clear that it was worth the trouble. Having specific and concrete data on the usability of our system in its multiple iterations and versions has informed our wider theoretical perspective on the nature of use. But the flip side is that work on usability was greatly informed by the more general work that was carried out on work practices, journal use, and the changing information infrastructure. Each informs the other, and both are necessary for a clear picture of the emerging phenomena of digital libraries.

NOTES

[1] All members of the Social Science Team have contributed to this paper as well. We thank S. Leigh Star, Emily Ignacio, Robert Sandusky, Cecelia Merkel, Eric Larson, Rebecca Engsberg, Madonnalisa Gonzales.
[2] DeLIver is available at http://dli.grainger.uiuc.edu/deliver.htm
[3] For further information on the work of the Illinois DLI Project Social Science Team, see our Web site at http://anshar.grainger.uiuc.edu/dlisoc/socsci_site/index.html.

REFERENCES

Bishop, A. P. (1998a). Logins amd bailouts: Measuring access, use, and success in digital libraries. *Journal of Electronic Publishing, 4*(2). Retrieved October 12, 1999 from the World Wide Web: http://www.press.umich.edu/jep/04-02/bishop.html.
Bishop, A. P. (1998b). Digital libraries and knowledge disaggregation: The use of journal article components. In *DL '98: Proceedings of the 3rd ACM International Conference on Digital Libraries* (pp. 29-39). New York: ACM.
Bishop, A. P. (Comp.). (1996). *Libraries, people, and change: A research forum on digital libraries* (Proceedings of the 38th Allerton Park Institute held October 27-29, 1996). Retrieved October 12, 1999 from the World Wide Web: http://edfu.lis.uiuc.edu/allerton/96/.

Bishop, A. P. (Comp.). (1995). *How we do user-centered design and evaluation of digital libraries: A methodological forum* (Proceedings of the 37th Allerton Park Institute held October 29-31, 1995). Retrieved October 12, 1999 from the World Wide Web: http://edfu.lis.uiuc.edu/allerton/95/.

Bishop, A. P., & Star, S. L. (1996). Social informatics for digital library infrastructure and use. In M. E. Williams (Ed.), *Annual review of information science and technology* (vol. 31, pp. 301-401). Medford, NJ: Information Today.

Borghuis, M.; Brinckman, H.; Fischer, A.; Hunter, K.; van der Loo, E.; ter Mors, R.; Mostert, P.; & Zijlstra, J. (1996). *TULIP: Final report.* New York: Elsevier Science.

Entlich, R.; Garson, L.; Lesk, M.; Normore, L.; Olsen, J.; Weibel, S. (1997). Making a digital library: The contents of the CORE project. *TOIS, 15*(2), 103-123.

Garvey, W., & Griffith, B. (1980). *Scientific communication: Its role in the conduct of research and creation of knowledge* (Key Papers in Information Science). White Plains, NY: Knowledge and Industry Publications.

Ignacio, E. N.; Neumann, L. J.; & Sandusky, R. J. (1995). *John and Jane Q. Engineer: What about our users?* Unpublished internal report. Retrieved October 12, 1999 from the World Wide Web: http://anshar.grainger.uiuc.edu/dlisoc/socsci_site/J.J.Q.Engineer.html.

Lancaster, F. W. (1995). Needs, demands and motivations in the use of sources of information. *Journal of Information, Communication, and Library Science, 1*(3), 3-19.

Monk, A.; Wright, P.; Haber, J.; & Davenport, L. (1993). *Improving your human-computer interface: A practical technique.* New York: Prentice Hall.

Neumann, L. J., & Ignacio, E. N. (1998). *Trial and error as a learning strategy in system use.* Unpublished paper presented at the American Society for Information Science Annual Conference held October 26-29, Pittsburgh, PA.

Neumann, L., & Star, S. L. (1996). Making infrastructure: The dream of a common language. In *Proceedings of the participatory design conference 1996* (PDC '96). Cambridge, MA: Computer Professionals for Social Responsibility/ACM.

Pinelli, T. (1991). The information-seeking habits and practices of engineers. *Science and Technologies Libraries, 11*(3), 5-25.

Star, S. L.; Bowker, G. C.; & Neumann, L. J. (forthcoming). *Transparency beyond the individual level of scale: Convergence between information artifacts and communities of practice.* In A. P. Bishop, N. Van House, & B. Butterfield (Eds.), *Digital library use: Social practice in design and evaluation.* Cambridge, MA: MIT Press.

Semantic Issues for Digital Libraries

Hsinchun Chen

INTRODUCTION

In this era of the Internet and distributed multimedia computing, new and emerging classes of information systems applications have swept into the lives of office workers and everyday people. New applications ranging from digital libraries, multimedia systems, geographic information systems, collaborative computing to electronic commerce, virtual reality, and electronic video arts and games have created tremendous opportunities for information and computer science researchers and practitioners.

As the applications become more overwhelming, pressing, and diverse, several well-known information retrieval (IR) problems have become even more urgent in this "network-centric" information age. Information overload, a result of the ease of information creation and rendering via the Internet and the World Wide Web, has become more evident in people's lives (e.g., even stockbrokers and elementary school students, heavily exposed to various WWW search engines, are versed in such IR terminology as "recall" and "precision"). Significant variations of database formats and structures, the richness of information media (text, audio, and video), and an abundance of multilingual information content also have created severe information interoperability problems—structural interoperability, media interoperability, and multilingual interoperability.

The conventional approaches to addressing information overload and information interoperability problems are manual in nature, requiring human experts as information intermediaries to create knowledge structures and/or ontologies (e.g., the National Library of Medicine's Unified Medical Language System project, UMLS). As information content and collections become even larger and more dynamic, we believe a system-aided bottom-up artificial intelligence (AI) approach is needed. By applying scalable techniques developed in various AI subareas (and related fields) such as image segmentation and indexing, voice recognition, natural language processing, neural networks, machine learning, clustering and categorization, and intelligent agents, we can provide an alternative system-aided approach to addressing both information overload and information interoperability.

FEDERAL INITIATIVES: DIGITAL LIBRARIES AND OTHERS

The Information Infrastructure Technology and Applications (IITA) Working Group, the highest level of the country's National Information Infrastructure (NII) technical committee, held an invited workshop in May 1995 to define a research agenda for digital libraries (see http://Walrus.Stanford.EDU/diglib/pub/reports/iitadlw/main.html). The shared vision is an entire net of distributed repositories where objects of any type can be searched within and across different indexed collections (Schatz & Chen, 1996). In the short term, technologies must be developed to search transparently across these repositories handling any variations in protocols and formats (i.e., addressing structural interoperability (Paepcke et al., 1996). In the long term, technologies must be developed to handle the variations in content and meanings transparently as well. These requirements are steps along the way toward matching the concepts requested by users with objects indexed in collections (Schatz, 1997).

The ultimate goal, as described in the IITA report, is the Grand Challenge of Digital Libraries:

> deep semantic interoperability—the ability of a user to access, consistently and coherently, similar (though autonomously defined and managed) classes of digital objects and services, distributed across heterogeneous repositories, with federating or mediating software compensating for site-by-site variations. . . . Achieving this will require breakthroughs in description as well as retrieval, object interchange, and object retrieval protocols. Issues here include the definition and use of metadata and its capture or computation from objects (both textual and multimedia), the use of computed descriptions of objects, federation and integration of heterogeneous repositories with disparate semantics, clustering and automatic hierarchical organization of information, and algorithms for automatic rating, ranking, and evaluation of information quality, genre, and other properties. (p. 5)

Attention to semantic interoperability has prompted several of the NSF/DARPA/NASA funded large-scale digital library initiative (DLI) projects to explore various artificial intelligence, statistical, and pattern recognition techniques—e.g., concept spaces and category maps in the Illinois project (Schatz et al., 1996), textile and word sense disambiguation in the Berkeley project (Wilensky, 1996), voice recognition in the CMU project (Wactlar et al., 1996), and image segmentation and clustering in the UCSB project (Manjunath & Ma, 1996).

The ubiquity of online information as perceived by U. S. leaders (e.g., "Information President" Clinton and "Information Vice President" Gore) as well as the general public and recognition of the importance of turning information into knowledge have continued to push information and computer science researchers toward developing scalable artificial intelligence techniques for other emerging information systems applications.

In the Santa Fe Workshop on Distributed Knowledge Work Environments: Digital Libraries held in March 1997, the panel of digital library researchers and practitioners suggested three areas of research for the planned Digital Library Initiative-2 (DLI-2): system-centered issues, collection-centered issues, and user-centered issues. Scalability, interoperability, adaptability and durability, and support for collaboration are the four key research directions under system-centered issues. System interoperability, syntactic (structural) interoperability, linguistic interoperability, temporal interoperability, and semantic interoperability are recognized by leading researchers as the most challenging and rewarding research areas (see http://www.si.umich.edu/SantaFe/).

In a new NSF Knowledge Networking (KN) initiative, a group of domain scientists and information systems researchers was invited to a workshop on distributed heterogeneous knowledge networks at Boulder, Colorado, in May 1997. Scalable techniques to improve semantic bandwidth and knowledge bandwidth are considered among the priority research areas described in the KN report (see http://www.scd.ucar.edu/info/KDI/).

The Knowledge Networking initiative focuses on the integration of knowledge from different sources and domains across space and time. Modern computing and communications systems provide the infrastructure to send bits anywhere, anytime, and in mass quantities—"radical connectivity." But connectivity alone cannot assure: (1) useful communication across disciplines, languages, and cultures; (2) appropriate processing and integration of knowledge from different sources, domains, and nontext media; (3) efficacious activity and arrangements for teams, organizations, classrooms, or communities working together over distance and time; or (4) a deepening understanding of the ethical, legal, and social implications of new developments in connectivity but not interactivity and integration. KN research aims to move beyond connectivity to achieve new levels of interactivity, increasing semantic bandwidth, knowledge bandwidth, activity bandwidth, and cultural bandwidth among people, organizations, and communities.

SEMANTIC ISSUES FOR DIGITAL LIBRARIES

Among the artificial intelligence techniques (and the affiliated statistical and pattern recognition fields) that are considered scale and domain independent, the following classes of algorithms and methods have been examined and subjected to experimentation in various digital libraries, multimedia databases, and information science applications.

OBJECT RECOGNITION, SEGMENTATION, AND INDEXING

The most fundamental techniques in IR involve identifying key features in objects. For example, automatic indexing and natural language processing (e.g., noun phrase extraction or object type tagging) are frequently used to extract automatically meaningful keywords or phrases from texts (Salton, 1989).

Texture, color, or shape-based indexing and segmentation techniques are often used to identify images (Manjunath & Ma, 1996). For audio and video applications, voice recognition, speech recognition, and scene segmentation techniques can be used to identify meaningful descriptors in audio or video streams (Wactler et al., 1996).

SEMANTIC ANALYSIS

Several classes of techniques have been used for semantic analysis of texts or multimedia objects. Symbolic machine learning (e.g., ID3, version space), graph-based clustering, and classification (e.g., Ward's hierarchical clustering), statistics-based multivariate analyses (e.g., latent semantic indexing, multidimensional scaling, regressions), artificial neural network-based computing (e.g., back propagation networks, Kohonen self-organizing maps), and evolution-based programming (e.g., genetic algorithms) are among the popular techniques (Chen, 1995). In this information age, we believe these techniques will serve as good alternatives for processing, analyzing, and summarizing large amounts of diverse and rapidly changing multimedia information.

KNOWLEDGE REPRESENTATIONS

The results from a semantic analysis process could be represented in the form of semantic networks, decision rules, or predicate logic. Many researchers have attempted to integrate such results with existing human-created knowledge structures such as ontologies, subject headings, or thesauri. Spreading activation-based inferencing methods are often used to traverse various large-scale knowledge structures (Chen & Ng, 1995).

HUMAN-COMPUTER INTERACTIONS AND
INFORMATION VISUALIZATION

One of the major trends in almost all emerging information systems applications is the focus on user-friendly, graphical, and seamless HCI. The Web-based browsers for texts, images, and videos have raised user expectations on the rendering and manipulation of information. Recent advances in development languages and platforms such as Java, OpenGL, and VRML and the availability of advanced graphical workstations at affordable prices have also made information visualization a promising area for research (DeFanti & Brown, 1990). Several of the digital library research teams, including Arizona/Illinois, Xerox PARC, Berkeley, and Stanford, are pushing the boundary of visualization techniques for dynamic displays of large-scale information collections.

ILLINOIS DLI SEMANTIC RESEARCH: AN EXAMPLE

In this section, we present an example of selected semantic retrieval and analysis techniques developed by The University of Arizona Artificial Intelligence Lab (AI Lab) for the Illinois DLI project. For detailed technical discussions, readers are referred to Chen et al. (1996, 1998). A textual semantic analysis pyramid was developed by The University of Arizona AI Lab to assist in semantic indexing, analysis, and visualization of textual documents. The pyramid, as depicted in Figure 1, consists of four layers of techniques, from bottom to top: noun phrase indexing, concept association, automatic categorization, and advanced visualization.

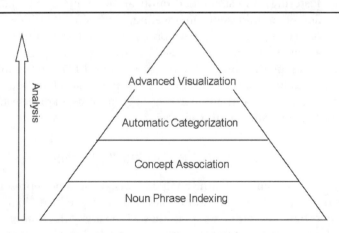

Figure 1. A Textual Semantic Analysis Pyramid

- Noun phrase indexing aims to identify concepts (grammatically correct noun phrases) from a collection for term indexing. It begins with a text tokenization process to separate punctuation and symbols. It follows by part-of-speech-tagging (POST) using variations of the Brill tagger and thirty-plus grammatic noun phrasing rules. Figure 2 shows an example of tagged noun phrases for a simple sentence (the system is referred to as AZ Noun Phraser). For example, "interactive navigation" is a noun phrase that consists of an adjective (A) and a noun (N).

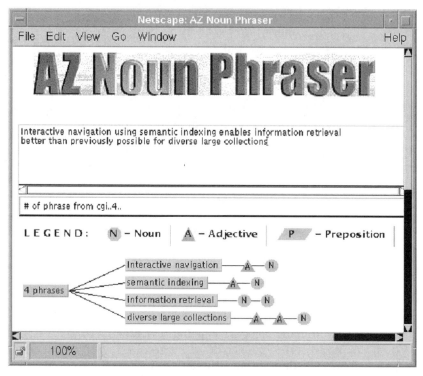

Figure 2. Tagged Noun Phrases

- Concept Association: Concept association attempts to generate weighted, contextual concept (term) association in a collection to assist in concept-based associative retrieval. It adopts several heuristic term weighting rules and a weighted co-occurrence analysis algorithm. Figure 3 shows the associated terms for "information retrieval" in a sample collection of project reports of the DARPA/ITO Program–TP (Term Phrase) such as "R system," "information retrieval engine," "speech collection," and so on.

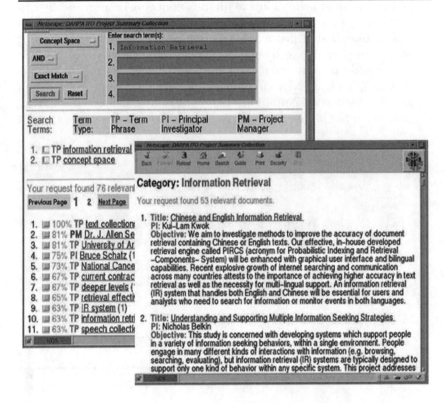

Figure 3. Associated Terms for "Information Retrieval"

- Automatic Categorization: A category map is the result of performing a neural network-based clustering (self-organizing) of similar documents and automatic category labeling. Documents that are similar (in noun phrase terms) to each other are grouped together in a neighborhood on a two-dimensional display. As shown in the colored jigsaw-puzzle display in Figure 4, each colored region represents a unique topic that contains similar documents. Topics that are more important often occupy larger regions. By clicking on each region, a searcher can browse documents grouped in that region. An alphabetical list that is a summary of the 2D result is also displayed on the left-hand side of Figure 4—e.g., Adaptive Computing System (thirteen documents), Architectural Design (nine documents), and so on.
- Advanced Visualization: In addition to the 2D display, the same clustering result can also be displayed in a 3D helicopter fly-through landscape as shown in Figure 5, where cylinder height represents the number of documents in each region. Similar documents are grouped in a

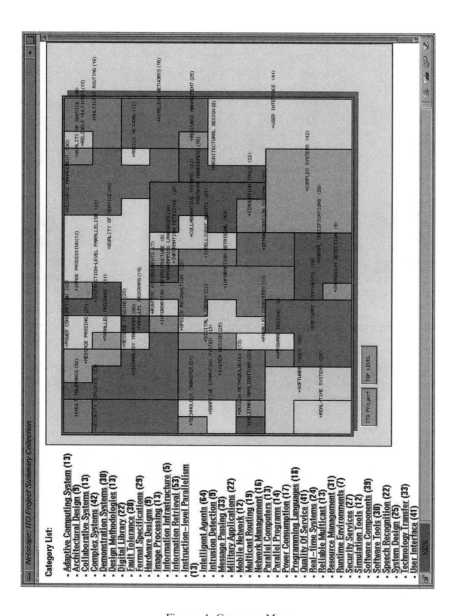

Figure 4. Category Map

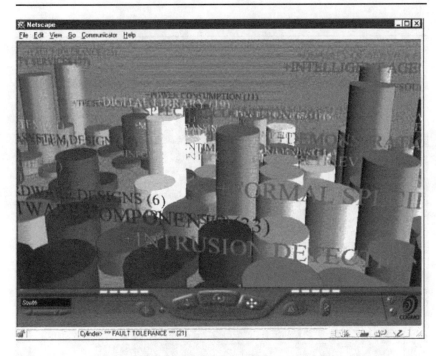

Figure 5. VRML Interface for Category Map

same-colored region. Using a VRML plug-in (COSMO player), a searcher is then able to "fly" through the information landscape and explore interesting topics and documents. Clicking on a cylinder will display the underlying clustered documents.

DISCUSSIONS

The techniques discussed above were developed in the context of the Illinois DLI project, especially for the engineering domain. The techniques appear scalable and promising. We are currently in the process of fine-tuning these techniques for collections of different sizes and domains.

ACKNOWLEDGMENT

This project was funded primarily by: (1) NSF/CISE "Concept-based Categorization and Search on Internet: A Machine Learning, Parallel 6 Computing Approach," NSF IRI9525790, 1995-1998, and (2) NSF/ARPA/ NASA Illinois Digital Library Initiative project, "Building the Interspace: Digital Library Infrastructure for a University Engineering Community," NSF IRI9411318, 1994-1998.

REFERENCES

Chen, H. (1995). Machine learning for information retrieval: Neural networks, symbolic learning, and genetic algorithms. *Journal of the American Society for Information Science, 46*(3), 194-216.

Chen, H.; Houston, A. L.; Sewell, R. R.; & Schatz, B. R. (1998). Internet browsing and searching: User evaluations of category map and concept space techniques. *Journal of the American Society for Information Science, 49*(7), 582-603.

Chen, H., & Ng, D. T. (1995). An algorithmic approach to concept exploration in a large knowledge network (automatic thesaurus consultation): Symbolic branch-and-bound versus connectionist Hopfield net activation. *Journal of the American Society for Information Science, 46*(5), 348-369.

Chen, H.; Schatz, B. R.; Ng, T. D.; Martinez, T. D.; Kirchhoff, A. J.; & Lin, C. (1996). A parallel computing approach to creating engineering concept spaces for semantic retrieval: The Illinois Digital Library Initiative Project. *IEEE Transactions on Pattern Analysis and Machine Intelligence, 18*(8), 771-782.

DeFanti, T., & Brown, M. (1990). *Visualization: Expanding scientific and engineering research opportunities.* New York: IEEE Computer Society Press.

Lynch, C., & Garcia-Molina, H. (1995). *Interoperability, scaling, and the digital libraries agenda.* Unpublished report on the May 18-19, 1995 IITA Digital Libraries Workshop, August 22, 1995.

Manjunath, B. S., & Ma, W. Y. (1996). Texture features for browsing and retrieval of image data. *IEEE Transactions on Pattern Analysis and Machine Intelligence, 18*(8), 837-841.

McCray, A. T., & Hole, W. T. (1990). The scope and structure of the first version of the UMLS semantic network. In *Proceedings of the 14th Annual Symposium on Computer Applications in Medical Care* (held November 4-7, 1990, Los Alamitos, California, Institute of Electrical and Electronics Engineers) (pp. 126-130). Waltham, MA: IEEE.

Paepcke, A.; Cousins, S. B.; Garcia-Molino, H.; Hasson, S. W.; Ketchpel, S. P.; Roscheisen, M.; & Winograd, T. (1996). Using distributed objects for digital library interoperability. *IEEE Computer, 29*(5), 61-69.

Salton, G. (1989). *Automatic text processing.* Reading, MA: Addison-Wesley Publishing Company, Inc.

Schatz, B. R. (1997). Information retrieval in digital libraries: Bring search to the net. *Science, 275*(January 17), 327-334.

Schatz, B. R., & Chen, H. (1996). Building large-scale digital libraries. *IEEE Computer, 29*(5), 22-27.

Schatz, B. R.; Mischo, B.; Cole, T.; Hardin, J.; Bishop, A. P.; & Chen, H. (1996). Federating repositories of scientific literature. *IEEE Computer, 29*(5), 28-36.

Wactlar, H. D.; Kanade, T.; Smith, M. A.; & Stevens, S. M. (1996). Intelligent access to digital video: Informedia project. *IEEE Computer, 29*(5), 46-53.

Wilensky, R. (1996). Toward work-centered digital information services. *IEEE Computer, 29*(5), 37-45.

TECHNOLOGY TRANSFER IN A PUBLIC UNIVERSITY

Robert Wedgeworth

INTRODUCTION

Technology transfer, as it will be used in this article, refers to the transformation of research information into marketable products and services. Although it occurs most frequently within a corporate context—within and among corporations—increasingly it occurs between university research groups and commercial entities. It is the latter context that is of concern here.

The principal purpose of this discussion is to share some experience and a perspective on technology transfer. As we move further into the digital era, more products and services will be developed to assist and support users across all disciplines. Since the bulk of the experience with the transfer of information technologies has occurred within the sciences, more will have to be done to share that experience as faculty and researchers in the humanities and the arts become involved. Perhaps our experience in the Digital Library Initiative (DLI) will assist in that development.

ORIGINS OF A TECHNOLOGY TRANSFER EFFORT

From the inception of the Digital Library Initiative project at the University of Illinois (UIUC), there was a commitment to continue the testbed of scientific information beyond the life of the project. Prospects for handling scientific journal articles in a digital environment is of fundamental and continuing interest to research libraries. Conversations involving the principal investigator and the university librarian focused on several prospects for financing the continuation of the testbed, including subsequent research grants, special funding from the university, and support from industrial sponsors.

Toward the end of the second year of the four-year research grant, it was clear that there was considerable interest in transferring to the scientific communications industry the experience and knowledge gained in building electronic repositories. We were aware that even the largest of the scientific journal publishers were struggling to develop such repositories. It is a problem of both financial resources and technical expertise (Elsevier finally contracted with Microsoft). We also had reason to believe that our project sponsors (NSF, NASA, and DARPA) would look favorably upon a successful technology transfer component to the DLI. It was with this motivation that I, as university librarian, took the lead in consultation with the principal investigator to define and initiate a technology transfer project.

THE DIGITAL LIBRARY INITIATIVE EXPERIENCE

The operating assumption was that since the DLI project was such a highly specialized area with only modest prospects for commercialization, it would not be of major interest to an established corporation. We then became aware of a small group of potential investors who had some experience with biotech startups and who were interested in related opportunities.

On a parallel track, we initiated conversations with the university office responsible for technology transfer in order to cultivate their interest and to get advice on how to proceed. We organized a meeting of the potential investors and the relevant university officer, which resulted in plans to investigate the potential for a startup company while exploring prospects for a licensing agreement with the university. After six months of efforts to define the technologies to be licensed and to develop a business plan for a startup company, it became apparent that the process was ill-advised. Through a miscommunication, several steps required by the university had not been taken (better to say "had been omitted?") and the process had to be redefined.

Although, by this time, a startup company had been formed and incorporated in Delaware, two things had to occur before the university would be willing to proceed. First, there had to be an independent review of the technologies involved including a determination of their potential value as well as the advisability of choosing a startup company as the strategy for transferring the technologies to industry.

Second, a conflict of interest (COI) review had to be completed and a conflict management plan, if necessary, had to be approved. Although a COI review had been anticipated, there was some confusion within the university as to who initiates the process since clearly the parties in potential conflict do not perform the review themselves. Approximately eighteen months after the initial conversations between the investors and the university, the two required steps were completed successfully. The potential licensing agreement is still in negotiation. As a result of this experience what had we learned?

TECHNOLOGY TRANSFER: A CONTACT SPORT

The literature focusing on technology transfer identifies five sequential steps that form the framework for successful technological transfer:

1. shared understanding of what can be;
2. trust among principals established and maintained;
3. distinct and complementary roles;
4. willingness to share knowledge; and
5. mutual benefits defined and maintained.

Shared Understanding

The lack of a shared understanding among the concerned parties—the research group, the university, and the investors—as to the importance and urgency of the project and how it could affect the scientific communication industry, inhibited a reasonable pace in the process. More formal as well as informal meetings among the parties would have been helpful.

Building Trust

Protracted delays and changes in key university personnel, causing fits and starts in the process, hampered the building of trust among the parties. The natural uneasiness within the academic culture about commercial ventures, especially in a public university, stimulated some confusion within the investor group as to what the university wanted and caused suspicion within the research group as to whether their interests were being protected adequately.

Role Definition

Unplanned developments within the investor group resulted in the university librarian becoming the President *pro tem* of the company and led to some confusion of roles within the university that inhibited communications (Is it the President or the University Librarian?). Although this was understood to be a temporary arrangement in order to facilitate development of the business plan, emphasizing its temporary nature tended to undermine confidence in the new venture, while understating it raised additional conflict of interest issues.

Willingness to Transfer Information

There was a willingness to share information for a technology transfer project among the researchers. However, the process of assigning responsibility for the creation of certain prototype features became such a formal and legalistic process that it tended to interfere with the normal workflow within the group and may have created a more competitive atmosphere by stimulating a search for patentable technologies.

WHO BENEFITS?

The lack of a strong market demand for a product or service for which there is little precedent made it difficult to project the benefits to all parties involved.

CONCLUSION

What seems clearer in hindsight is that neither policies, nor processes, nor technological understandings, nor legal and contractual matters, nor economic incentives are at the heart of technology transfer. It is relationships.

Carefully drafted documents do not build trust. In fact, the early introduction of formal legalistic discussions inhibits the building of trust as individuals instinctively become more cautious about what they discuss openly.

Academics do not naturally accept relationships with commercial ventures. Even though the greater proportion of the university budget in public universities increasingly comes from non-public sources, there is limited experience with commercial ventures other than grants and contracts. As the prospect for technology spreads across more disciplines, what appears to be needed is an articulated effort to build a better understanding of such ventures and allay fears of faculty that their research objectives might be distorted.

University Technology Web Sites

In order to get a sense of how major public universities were focusing on technology transfer, I toured a number of technology office Web sites linked to Rice University (www.crpc.rice.edu/university). The questions that were of primary interest were:

- Which sites display intellectual property policies?
- Which sites list research areas available for licensing?
- Which sites give directions for startup companies?
- Which sites display conflict of interest policies?
- Which sites explicitly encourage technology transfer?

Among the CIC universities, all but two prominently display intellectual property policies. Eight of the thirteen CIC campuses list primary research areas that are available for licensing. Six of the CIC campuses give directions for how to proceed in developing startup companies with their institutions. Six of the CIC campuses display conflict of interest policies. Eight of the CIC campuses explicitly encourage technology transfer. Two of the campuses did not have technology center Web sites.

What this brief look does not indicate is how difficult it is to get access to this information if you begin at the university's general Web site. The significance of the intellectual property and conflict of interest policies is that many questions can be answered readily by access to such documents. Directions for startup companies is an indication that there has been systematic thought given to how a university wishes to guide such ventures and avoids having to negotiate each new venture from a clean slate. Limited personnel in both legal and technical areas of technology transfer would suggest that an articulated body of information that serves both the experienced researcher and the novice will be necessary to constrain the growth of personnel for technology transfer counseling and advisory services. More importantly, it is an explicit demonstration of the importance of technology to the institution and how far it is willing to go to encourage it.

A Publisher's Perspective
More Successes Than Failures

Tim Ingoldsby

The University of Illinois Digital Library Initiative (DLI) has offered scientific publishers a unique opportunity to participate in a digital library research project oriented toward answering research questions of great interest to publishers. This discussion will represent the views of the publishing partners who contributed to the DLI project. Participation was very rewarding for the publishers and the individuals who attended the annual project briefings and learned from the renowned Illinois research team.

In preparing this article, a review was performed of quarterly reports submitted to the National Science Foundation since the project began in 1994. Also consulted were other publishers who contributed materials to the project to obtain their impressions of the preliminary outcomes of the project. I am grateful for their contributions.

AMERICAN INSTITUTE OF PHYSIC'S HISTORY IN THE PROJECT

When the University of Illinois was awarded one of the six DLI grants in 1994, the American Institute of Physics (AIP) was not listed as a partner.[1] However, soon after the announcements, a session was held at the American Association for the Advancement of Science's (AAAS) annual meeting featuring the principal investigators for each of the awardees. During that AAAS meeting, I had a chance encounter with Bruce Schatz in the exhibit area, where I was demonstrating AIP's recently released pioneering online physics journal, *Applied Physics Letters Online*.[2] The journal was a weekly letters compilation and had been available in full text SGML since October 1994. Schatz was having trouble finding publishers for the DLI project that could contribute science or engineering journals in SGML. He invited AIP to join the project, and we enthusiastically accepted. Since *APL Online* was a research project anyway, we saw this as an opportunity to get two results from a single development project. We would be able to learn from the successes and failures of each system and approach.

Since we already had a large body of some 1,000 valid SGML articles, *APL Online* became the first journal to be incorporated into the DLI system. This was extremely valuable for AIP, as we became the first publisher to benefit from the careful analysis of our SGML and the successes and failures encountered by the project team as they crafted a powerful SGML-based search and retrieval system. We were so pleased with the early results that we offered two additional journals in SGML[3] to the project in mid-1996. The power of our SGML implementation was further validated when these two new journals were incorporated into the project with almost zero additional effort.

By this time, the American Institute of Physics had made a business decision to establish our own online journal service and move all sixteen of the AIP physics journals online by January 1997. As a result of this extensive project, our ability to perform additional research in house was drastically reduced, and the DLI became our primary research and development center. Much of the look and feel of the user interface for our own service came from lessons learned in the DLI project. Another result of our preoccupation with our new online service was our decision to provide some financial support to the DLI project so they would continue to perform some routine SGML production services that we had earlier agreed to take over so the project staff could concentrate on bringing the materials submitted by other publishers online.

Another aspect of the financial agreement with the DLI was the development of a distributed repository at AIP. By mid-1997, our Online Journal Publishing Service (OJPS) was stable and fairly robust, and we were anxious to model a distributed database environment, which we believe to be one of the likely eventual environments for the online research environment. We agreed to host the first distributed repository for the project. As this article was being written, the DLI staff was replicating the database structure and was in the final stage of testing before AIP journals began to be searched on our Woodbury, New York, server by users of the DLI system on the Urbana-Champaign campus.

REVIEW OF THE RESEARCH: TESTBED

From a practical standpoint, the development of the testbed and DLI's demonstration that it is possible to use SGML from many publishers in a single coherent system is the project's most significant accomplishment. DLI research programmers had to develop a system that could receive

SGML files conforming to at least six different DTDs and merge them into a uniformly searchable system. The volume of material must have been staggering for researchers that were used to small test databases. The American Institute of Physics was delivering fifty to sixty articles weekly, and the American Physical Society an average of sixty to seventy more. The programmers developed auto-processing systems that resulted in their ability to add new issues to the collection in a matter of a few hours. Many weeks I have found a new issue of *APL Online* available on the DLI even before it is mounted to our own OJPS even though both services receive the material at essentially the same time and the DLI has to process full articles, whereas our OJPS only deals with bibliographic information and abstracts. The OpenText search engine selected by the project staff has been thoroughly tested, and practically every capability it provides has found a use in the DLI implementation.

The testbed group also made great strides in interface design. The American Institute of Physics recognized early in the project that the collaboration between the testbed group and the User Studies/Social Sciences team would produce a very functional interface design. The use of a custom client, developed with Visual Basic (VB) rapid prototyping tools, allowed frequent updates to the functionality in reaction to user preferences. However, the reliance on VB also had a drawback—i.e., the client needed to be installed on every workstation every time it was updated. The custom program approach also was contradictory to users' overwhelming preference for a standard Web browser. Perhaps the project staff stayed with the custom client too long, but the Web DeLIver client that was developed in late 1997 benefitted from the rapid prototyping phase.

The final validation of the excellent work of the testbed group came with the announcement that DARPA was providing a grant to continue the testbed for an additional three years. We expect to see additional accomplishments during this phase.

REVIEW OF THE RESEARCH: USER STUDIES

One of the hidden joys of this project has been the opportunity to interact with the User Studies group led by Ann Bishop at the University of Illinois at Urbana-Champaign. They have been a joy to work with, and AIP has drawn on their expertise for our own user studies. Publishers have much to learn from the social science aspects of this research. We often feel that we know what our customers *need,* but Bishop's research shows that we do not necessarily know what they *want.* We have applied what we have learned from the User Studies group's use of various tools and feedback-gathering strategies to our own interactions with our customers. Their interview techniques have been very instructive. Another valuable insight has come from their instrumentation of the client to gather feedback when it is fresh in the mind of the user. Bishop's group has contributed much of value to the process of understanding how researchers approach their tasks. Now that the testbed is to be extended to the wider Committee on Institutional Cooperation (CIC) community, user studies will have even more validity based on the expansion of the test population.

REVIEW OF THE RESEARCH: SEMANTIC RESEARCH

This group, led by Bruce Schatz and Hsinchun Chen, has produced the most forward reaching "Star Wars" research results. Their work is definitely more "research" than "development" but, even so, they have produced results that have meaning. They are leading the way to the future, even though, for most publishers, their efforts are beyond our event horizon at the present—with one exception. The IODyne research tool developed by Eric Johnson is a concrete example of the type of search aid that will assist the scientific research community in the near future. We at AIP are very excited about applying the concepts used by Johnson in doing keyword searches to enable more effective use of AIP's Physics and Astronomy Classification Scheme (PACS) codes in searching physics research.

Schatz and Chen have excelled in educating publishers about the obstacles to semantic retrieval. They have also found interesting uses for supercomputers—e.g., building concept spaces for large research collections. They have also enhanced the simplistic approaches of single word searches by developing noun phrase algorithms that improve the quality of machine searching results. They are also doing the fundamental research with concepts such as self-organizing maps and algorithms for automatic categorization. Here is an area where research performed in one of the six digital library projects has applicability and benefit for all of the other projects as well.

REVIEW OF THE RESEARCH: SYSTEM EVALUATION

This final component of the research for the DLI project has been the least visible in terms of accomplishments and continuing efforts. It is possible that much of the reason for this has been the way that the world has changed during the past four years. It is instructive to read the original proposal in which NCSA's Mosaic was expected to be the vehicle for much of the information delivery. It is sad to note that most of the "newbies" to the Web have never even heard of Mosaic, the compelling application that drove the rapid expansion of the World Wide Web. Even so, I have been personally disappointed by the lack of contributions to this project by the NCSA and Computer Science group. The quarterly reports of the project document the diminishing impact and value of this aspect of the project.

HOW ONE PUBLISHER HAS PROFITED FROM INVOLVEMENT IN THE DLI PROJECT

The American Institute of Physics has already begun to profit from our participation in the DLI through the process of technology transfer. Our efforts to develop the AIP OJPS have profited from the research activities of the DLI project. Our search interface, in particular, owes much of its heritage to the Visual Basic client prototyping. SGML to HTML conversion routines developed at AIP have been improved by discussions with DLI staff. The DLI problems with the display of SGML full-text articles, particularly the problems with rendering special characters and mathematical formulas, convinced us to remain with PDF as our primary full text "deliverable" for now.[4] Our service has also attracted other society customers. We now deliver thirty-six journals through our Online Journal Publishing Service. The awareness of our partnership with the DLI project has been cited by many societies as a factor in their decision to work with AIP's online service. Even so, it will be 1999 or later before the OJPS can deliver features that have been present in a research mode within the DLI project since 1997.

MAJOR SUCCESSES OF THE DLI PROJECT

In keeping with the theme of this conference, there was an attempt to identify the key successes and disappointments of the project. Clearly, the development of a "proof of concept" cross-publisher large-scale federated repository is the DLI's greatest achievement. At least until sometime in 1999, the DLI testbed will remain the largest sci-tech SGML article collection in the entire world. This testbed is beginning to deliver the promise of SGML: searchability across many titles, programmatic linking between articles published in journals of different publishers, and powerful fielded searching.

The DLI project has also made great strides in achieving a functional interface. This interface now incorporates results gleaned from interviews and other diagnostic processes that define how scientists and engineers use journal articles in the research process. Schatz and Chen have also produced impressive achievements in advancing the quest for semantic federation. These strides will lead to systems that make such tools commonplace in the next decade.

MAJOR DISAPPOINTMENTS OF THE DLI PROJECT

While it would be too strong to call them "failures," there have been two significant disappointments regarding what had been proposed for the project. Clearly, the project has failed to deliver adequate display of SGML-based scientific literature. If SoftQuad's Panorama had worked as anticipated, AIP and other scientific publishers would be rushing to convert from PDF full-text delivery to SGML. This remains the most difficult problem for publishers and may require government support to solve.[5]

The other disappointment is the final size of the testbed and the user population that was proposed to interact with it. Instead of the 100,000 documents and 20,000 users promised in the original proposal, the final numbers will be closer to 50,000 documents and 1,000 users. The publishers participating in this project are perhaps most disappointed by this shortcoming. Our judgment is that the testbed group stayed with the Visual Basic client for perhaps six months too long, thereby not leaving enough time to expand the user community to its fullest possible extent. However, the follow-on DARPA grant should permit the achievement of both goals.

LOOKING TO THE FUTURE

For its part, the American Institute of Physics is looking forward to continued collaboration with the testbed and user studies groups through the DARPA grant and the establishment of an industrial partners program for publishers. We would like to see more journals added to the testbed and will offer all sixteen AIP journals (which have been in full-text SGML since the beginning of 1998) on the distributed repository at AIP. We want to see the testbed group turn its efforts to solving the SGML math display problem. If MathML emerges as a viable solution, tools will need to be developed to convert ISO12083 math markup into MathML markup. The special character aspect of the display problem is well on its way to being solved by the STIX font project[6] that recently submitted to the UNICODE standards body a proposal to add every character required for mathematics, physical sciences, and life sciences to the standard code set which is, or shortly will be, supported by every browser developer. We have also suggested to the testbed group the development of a joint DLI-2 proposal to address these issues and others that are being faced by the scientific and engineering research community.

ACKNOWLEDGMENTS

AIP wishes to take this opportunity to thank Bruce Schatz, Bill Mischo, Tim Cole, Ann Bishop, and their associates for offering us the opportunity to participate in a research project of this calibre. The cooperation between university and publishing has been beyond expectation.

NOTES

[1] The American Institute of Physics was a participant in the unfunded proposal, *Science Quest*, submitted by the University of Maryland.

[2] *Applied Physics Letters Online* was the first physics journal made available through OCLC's Electronic Journals Online program.

[3] *Journal of Applied Physics* and *Review of Scientific Instruments.*

[4] Results from our electronic journals online experience with OCLC also confirmed the difficulty of using HTML full text supplemented by GIFs of special characters and formulas.

[5] However, the recent development of the Extensible Markup Language (XML) standard, its widespread endorsement by browser and rendering software vendors, and (most importantly) the development of the Math Markup Language (MathML) standard written in XML offer perhaps the best hope for a solution to this serious problem.

[6] A project of major scientific publishers including AIP, APS, ACS, IEEE, AMS, and Elsevier Science.

Lessons Learned from Full-Text Journals at OCLC

Thomas B. Hickey

OCLC operates many services and programs for libraries, but the major ones are an online cataloging system, an interlibrary loan system, and a reference service. The reference service (FirstSearch) includes full-text databases as well as databases of abstracts and indexes. We currently serve more than 25,000 libraries, have more than 1,100 full-text with-graphics journals online, and the FirstSearch databases contain more than 250 million records.

We started working on full-text journals by examining new approaches to information display. We felt that there would be a gradual movement from the availability of only metadata electronically to the full text of reference works, journal articles, and finally books. We started investigating and working with Donald Kuth's Metafont and TeX as soon as they were available, even to the point of doing our own ports of the systems. In general, this is the progression we have seen, although the wide availability of journal articles has taken longer than we expected twenty years ago.

In the early 1980s, there were two main problems regarding electronic display of text: fonts and speed. Scientific text especially requires a large number of special characters (glyphs) that were not generally available. In fact, electronic versions of fonts were hardly available at all except for the dot matrix ones embedded in hardware such as displays and printers. Speed problems had several aspects. Communications speed was the worst—we were working with 1200-baud modems typically with very expensive ($1000+) 9600-baud modems gradually becoming available. Printing was restricted to machines that could support a bitmap image of a page and typically took 5 to 10 minutes/page to display. Display of a page on CRTs was faster but still could take ten seconds or more because of the lack of hardware support for special fonts and limited processing speeds.

The research department at OCLC has had two main projects with full-text journals. The first was Graph-Text (Hickey & Calabrese, 1985). We worked with American Chemical Society (ACS) journals obtained through Chemical Abstract Service (CAS). CAS had a very sophisticated system, developed in the 1970s, which stored their journals in structured records in a database at a time when most publishers had no concept of storing any sort of electronic version of their material. We took tapes of their articles in their database format, translated them into TeX, and then into TeX's standard device independent format, DVI, creating new glyphs as needed using Metafont. Since the graphics were not on the tapes, we scanned the original documents, cropped out the graphics, and linked those to the graphic callouts in the articles. Our first system relied totally on metadata for identification and selection. It batched requests for overnight downloading and printing since delivery of an article with its associated fonts and graphics could take up to half an hour over modems.

Before we tested the system in libraries, we decided that PCs had progressed to the point where display of the formatted text and graphics was possible interactively, so we revised and extended the system to do this. To avoid slow transmission speeds, we stored the data on CD-ROMs. To store the data, we devised our own directory structure since there was no standard method of storing files on CDs at the time. These were, of course, single speed CD readers with very slow seek speeds, but they were much faster than running the system remotely over modems. We used Hercules Graphic cards for display on 286 PCs and the first of the Canon laser printers for printing (Hickey & Handley, 1987). The system worked fairly well, but we were never satisfied with CD-ROMs as a delivery mechanism for journal articles. There tend to be too many of them and they tend to be out of date.

Our second major project worked with John Wiley & Son's *Kirk-Othmer Encyclopedia of Chemical Technology* (Hickey, 1988). We obtained this from them in a simple text format designed for loading into an ASCII database system. We translated this into SGML and used the SGML to drive TeX and indexing for the database. For our testing, we concentrated on a single volume of the twenty-four volume encyclopedia and successfully translated it. For display, we used a Wyse 700 display which offered black and white resolutions comparable to those on CRTs today. Unfortunately no window system was available to make display of articles easier, so again we were forced to write software, such as window management and character display, which today is taken for granted. Over the past fifteen to twenty years, we have seen the following progression in the delivery system and format of our data:

Delivery	*Format*
1200-9600 Baud Offline	TeX/DVI

CD-ROM	TeX/DVI
Online, proprietary client	SGML/TeX/DVI
Web Browsers	HTML
	PDF & Image

OCLC's first commercial venture in formatted full text was called Electronic Journals Online (EJO). This was a joint project with the American Association for the Advancement of Science and started with a new electronic journal, *Current Clinical Trials*. We wrote our own client for the display of the articles that were coded in SGML and translated using TeX into DVI. All the fonts used were developed in-house. EJO had several dozen journals mounted at its height, but we found working with the SGML too expensive. Each publisher's DTD and special formatting requirements simply took too much staff time to make the system affordable. When the economics of the system became apparent, OCLC revamped the system into Electronic Collections Online (ECO). ECO now has more than 1,100 journals online and often loads more than fifty new journals each month, a rate much higher than we could ever have reached with the earlier SGML system. Each of these journals is stored in Portable Document Format (PDF), a format devised by Adobe to eliminate many of the portability and rendering problems that their PostScript format has. We do minimal processing on the data to mount metadata about each journal, issue, and article and link it to the PDF files. The whole system is closer to OCLC's FirstSearch database model and is being completely integrated with the FirstSearch system.

We have been working on bringing electronic documents to users since before it was really feasible and have learned a few lessons along the way:

- *CD-ROM is not the same as telecom.* On the face of it, this sounds obvious, but we were surprised by some of the consequences. We used CD-ROMs to move data to the user instead of setting up modems seeing the CDs as a replacement for the network. We found in focus groups that librarians looked at the CDs much as they did books and journals that they acquired—they owned them. Any sort of per-use charges for items they had physical control over was much less acceptable than per-use charges for items obtained remotely.
- *Math, tables, and layout are 90 percent of the effort.* On a day-to-day basis, these things are what continue to absorb time. Of the three, math is probably the worst if it is a central part of the articles, but tables can become extraordinarily complex and long (e.g., we encountered a fifty-seven page table). In our production databases, we sidestepped most of the layout problems by separating graphics and tables from the text,

but the Graph-Text project tried to match or better the ACS layout and required substantial effort.

- *Production was as expensive as predicted.* One of the main objectives of our early research was to assess how expensive processing the material would be. We went ahead with production plans in spite of the projections of $5 to15/page and found that, even at higher volumes, these costs were difficult to reduce.

- *SGML helps but not much.* One of our hopes was that getting SGML from the publishers would result in dramatically lower costs. SGML did help. It made it possible to mount journals from publishers. But the math and tables are still there, SGML offers little help in the actual rendering of the text, and our costs to mount SGML journals were too high.

- *TeX is hard to beat.* TeX is not the perfect typesetting system, especially for material you would like to manage in large batches. It is amazing, however, that nearly twenty years later there is still nothing better at what it does.

- *Fonts remain a problem.* The use of PDF insulates us from this problem, but somewhere in the production stream, someone is struggling with yet another character that someone has dreamt up.

- *Publishers were not ready.* Not nearly as true now, but the amount of education and liaison necessary with each publisher was a significant part of EJO's cost structure. Each new publisher was expensive. We could not charge enough to recover our costs for this.

- *Users are harder to change than publishers.* Users in general were not particularly interested in electronic journals until they had experience with the Web and started getting familiar with using information in a networked environment.

- *Proprietary clients are wrong.* There are still people learning this one. Just the barrier of having to install software on each machine that might access a service is too high for a system providing access to scholarly journals. We explored several ways to better integrate our service into the Web before settling on the use of PDF and Adobe Acrobat (Hickey, 1994, 1995).

- *It is the data that matters.* Fancy interfaces are fine, and we spent much time developing, testing, and changing ours, but these are not the most important things. The data are important, and images of pages are fine for this. One feature that is needed is printing, and PDF does a wonderful job at this, even though reading most PDF documents on the screen is difficult at best.

- *End users are less worried about format than publishers.* We suspected this from the start, but publishers have a vested interest in making their material look as unique as possible, and a system that ignores this will face great resistance from publishers. Our systems did try to maintain these publisher distinctions, but these proved expensive.

Electronic journals now face a whole new set of problems. When we started, we had problems of communications, printing, processing speed, proprietary clients, unavailable fonts, and when to start developing a product. Now the problems are more pricing, licensing, archiving, integration of the digital and the physical, and standards to reduce costs and increase interoperability. It seems that we have accomplished more in the last five years than we did in the ten before that. I hope the same will be true for the next five.

REFERENCES

Hickey, T. B., & Calabrese, A. M. (1985). Electronic document delivery: OCLC's Prototype System. *Library HiTech, 4*(1), 65-71.

Hickey, T. B., & Handley, J. C. (1987). Interactive display of text and graphics on an IBM-PC. In A. H. Helal & J. W. Weiss (Eds.), *Impact of new information technology on international library cooperation* (Proceedings of the Essen Symposium held September 8-11, 1986 in Essen, West Germany) (pp. 137-149). Essen, West Germany: Essen University Library.

Hickey, T. B. (1989). Using SGML and TeX for an interactive chemical encyclopedia. In *National Online Meeting* (Proceedings of the tenth National Online Meeting held May 9-11, 1989 in New York) (pp. 187-195). Medford, NJ: Learned Information, Inc.

Hickey, T. B. (1994). Integrating Guidon with the World Wide Web. *Annual Review of OCLC Research.* Retrieved October 27, 1998 from the World Wide Web: http://www.oclc.org/oclc/research/publications/review94/part1/integuid.htm.

Hickey, T. B. (1995). Guidon Web: Applying Java to scholarly electronic journals. *Annual Review of OCLC Research.* Retrieved October 27, 1998 from the World Wide Web: http://www.oclc.org/oclc/research/publications/review95/part1/guidon.htm.

THE FUTURE OF ANNOTATION IN A DIGITAL (PAPER) WORLD

Catherine C. Marshall

If order-making in the large is part of the institutional mission of libraries, then order-making in the small—i.e., the informal work of annotating and organizing materials collected in the service of particular day-to-day work or pleasure—is part of the business of library patrons. This discussion focuses on just such activities; activities that stem from readers' engagements with texts, and possibly with each other, against a backdrop of real-world settings and practices. I hesitate to call digital library patrons *users*, since that is the word computer scientists tend to use to hide the characteristics of what we hope is a diverse population.[1]

In Robert McCrum's (1994) account of the annotations Graham Greene's biographers found as they looked through the books in his personal library, he writes: "Many writers have left much larger collections, but what is different about Greene's library is the wealth of personal annotation, reflecting a long and crowded life of writing, politics, travel, and friendship. Scattered along the margins and jotted on the flyleaves and endpapers of these books are thousands of meticulous handwritten notes and comments" (p. 46).

Four properties of this account of annotation stand out. First, Graham Greene's annotations are personal with no expectation of an audience beyond himself. Second, they are literally on the pages of the book, and as such have become part of his library. Third, they have crossed from a private space—his library—into a more public space—the hands of his biographers. Finally, they have lasting value. This characterizes a very particular kind of annotation.

My second example of a kind of annotation comes from Vannevar Bush's (1945) prescient description of hypertext:

> The owner of the memex, let us say, is interested in the origin and
> properties of the bow and arrow. . . . He has dozens of possibly perti-

nent books and articles in his memex. First he runs through an encyclopedia, finds an interesting but sketchy article, leaves it projected.
Next, in a history, he finds another pertinent item, and ties the two
together. Thus he goes, building a trail of many items. Occasionally
he inserts a comment of his own. . . .Thus he builds a trail of his
interest through the maze of materials available to him. (p. 107)

So again we're looking at personal annotation, but this time it is digital and serves to connect documents; the trails Bush describes are not
part of the documents themselves. Later in the article, they too will cross
into a more public space—in this case, the hands of a friend researching a
similar topic. However, by contrast to Greene's annotations, the move of
the memex owner's annotations from a wholly private to a shared space is
done intentionally. Again, the annotations have value beyond their original purpose.

The variety of types of annotations, and indeed range of interpretations of what an annotation is and how it functions in the world, provoked
me to lay out an initial set of dimensions to characterize what I've encountered so far. These dimensions are not intended to suggest dichotomous
classifications but rather to gently investigate why all annotations are not
created equal.

The first two, *formal/informal* and *explicit/implicit*, are distinctions of
form. Informal annotations, like Graham Greene's jottings in the fly leaves,
may be descriptive, but in a digital world, they are not necessarily
computationally tractable. On the other end of the spectrum, metadata
created according to a standard, using attribute-value pairs and a source
of authority, may be computationally tractable and a good way to promote
interoperability, but it may also be costly to create. To reduce the overhead of description, we may use methods of extracting more formal description from informal annotations. The explicitness of an annotation is
what allows us, as nonauthors, to interpret it. An exclamation point in the
margin of a technical manual may be cryptic; a note on the frontispiece of
Portrait of the Artist as a Young Man—"Most important epiphany, p. 47"—
makes a good deal more sense. Explicitness is thus crucially related to the
ultimate intelligibility of an annotation.

The second three—*writing/reading*, *extensive/intensive*, and *permanent/
transient*—have to do with the function of the annotation. In much of the
literature about readers-as-writers, readers are variously a force that de-
centralizes authority, or they may play a far more traditional role as an
engaged audience. This tension, explored by Moulthrop (1993), crucially
dictates the ultimate value of the annotations in relation to the primary
text. If we take extensive reading to be along the lines of what Bush's
memex user was doing, and intensive reading to be deep engagement
with a single text as exhibited in Graham Greene's personal library, another characteristic of annotations comes to light: is the annotation across

various works or within them? This dimension follows from the distinction Levy (1997) makes when he describes types of reading and attention. The permanence of the marks really comes to the foreground when we talk about "going digital" since the marks are now readily separable from the document, they are transferable from one digital copy to another, and they can be easily removed. They can now take on a life of their own or be removed at will.

Finally, the last two dimensions, *published/private* and *institutional/workgroup/individual* have to do with intentional and unintentional movement of annotated documents from one person's hands to another. Let us first take the published/private dimension. Graham Greene's annotations moved seamlessly from being private to being, in effect, published. It is this movement that is of the greatest interest as we move to digital media, since this kind of movement is now very clumsy compared to what we do with paper documents. I can mark on a paper I'm reading, and when you ask for it, unless I've written something dreadful in the margins and rush to erase it, you will be able to see it—and make what you will of it—when I hand you my copy. What will this be like in a digital world in which we can lift our own responses to a document off with ease before we pass it on? Institutional/workgroup/individual simply refers to the intended audience for the annotations. The original visions of hypertext, in particular those of Engelbart and Nelson, were fundamentally additive; documents and their commentary make up the docuverse.

To explore some of these dimensions, and to introduce some related technologies, three stories about annotation will be presented. The first is about intelligence analysts and the annotations and order they make in the course of interpreting document collections; the second concerns K-12 teachers and their students and their use of Web materials in the classroom; finally, the third begins with college students and the marks they make in their textbooks and ends with some implications for future efforts to create a digital library reading machine.

Before beginning, I would like to expose another, more hidden, agenda for this talk that is very much in line with the "successes and failures" theme of this workshop—i.e., most of the technologies that will be discussed are not first generation efforts. They are in each case *simplifications* of earlier technologies that were found to be unworkable given the constraints of work in the world.

INTELLIGENCE ANALYSTS AND THEIR NOTES

The first story is about intelligence analysts and the sense and order they make in the course of interpreting heterogeneous collections of materials. This story begins well over a decade ago, and even before that if my involvement with this user community as a technology developer is considered. In 1989, I had the opportunity to conduct a series of work practice studies of intelligence analysts in their offices at various sites around the Washington, DC, area.

Much of what was learned about the analysts came out of individual interviews coupled with observations in and around their workplace. At the time I was engaged in this study, analysts often covered the same "beat" for long periods of time and had considerable familiarity with specific geo-political regions and topics.

Some of what was observed was, in retrospect, unsurprising but useful. Analysts use annotations the way most experts do; they are resourceful gatherers of materials from different forms and different places, and they organize working materials in ways suitable for immediate use and for personal archival storage. Each of these annotation-related facets of their activities are described very briefly.

Analysts engaged in at least three kinds of annotation. The first was a product of an analyst's engagement with a particular document. Analysts marked on reprints, cables, and other paper documents using highlighters and pens; these markings included marginalia, highlighting, and underlines—in short, much of what one would encounter in the office. Analytic work is crucially integrative; as such, analysts did what they could to capture and explore the relationships among documents, including ordering and reordering the documents in piles according to different criteria (for example, a chronology of action or a chronology of when the documents crossed their desks). Because the analysts used a variety of different online resources, their monitors were framed by a clutter of post-its to remind them of the "how to" details.

The documents they used were heterogeneous both in source and in media. They would readily combine personal materials with workgroup files—some of the analysts in the study had explicit shared files, others would rely on mediated access to their colleagues' personal files—and institutional publications. They would also consult online news providers such as NEXIS, Dialog, Comline, and others. Because this study took place in 1989 and early 1990, Internet information resources were not yet a part of standard practice. Despite claims that collaboration was infrequent, the analysts consulted with each other freely, looking for corroboration, missing information, opinions, and so on. It was only when these consultations resulted in a co-authored analytic paper that they were institutionally acknowledged as collaboration.

The analysts used multiple means of organizing the materials that they would gather over the course of an analysis and over the course of their careers in government service. Most important for this discussion are the transient visible ways of organizing materials to task exigencies. These organizations were exploratory—for it matters the order in which documents are encountered and which documents are in spatial

juxtaposition—and highly fluid. The organization of materials for a particular analysis did not necessarily reflect a longer-term archiving strategy.
Analysts cited simple archiving schemas based on "people, places, and
things" or geographical regions as the way to make their files accessible
over the long term.

Other findings about annotations and use of materials were more
provocative, especially from the perspective of a system-builder. First of
all, note-taking per se was uncommon. Brief annotations and manipula-
tions of the physical documents mediated between reading and writing.
An analyst might write "wrong!" or "don't believe this" in the margin of a
document but not elaborate on the interpretation until he or she was
producing an analytic report. Our previous efforts had resulted in a system called NoteCards (Halasz et al., 1987), which assumed a real note-
taking model of the sort we all learn in school.

Much of the pre-writing interpretive activity took place using paper
and the phone. Cables and retrieval results were printed; borrowed materials were on paper, photographic paper, or involved physical media. Need-
less to say, this aspect of practice presents a real challenge for those interested in supporting a range of interpretive activities online.

Although many institutional initiatives have been aimed at automat-
ing upstream aspects of analytic practice—i.e., extracting useful tidbits of
information or visualizing immense document collections—analysts' sense-
making relied crucially on communion with their source materials—i.e.,
much of what they made of materials hinged on reading, skimming, and
otherwise manipulating individual documents. Anecdotally, this communion is illustrated in an analyst's story about "the dog that didn't bark," an
important insight he had gained by observing what was *missing* from a
document rather than from what was *in* it. A second example comes from
observations of an analyst who printed out source materials, marked key
passages with a highlighter, then typed them back into her computer. While
it is tempting to dismiss this as yet another interoperability problem (why
couldn't she just move the materials from one window/system to another?),
it is more likely that the act of retyping the content was critically important to gaining purchase on what was said.

Finally, the one finding that amplified the need for observation in
situ was the difference between what I saw and the unified institutional
story actually encountered. Organizations that spend substantial time reflecting on their own failures and successes, and telling "how we work"
stories, have well-crafted narratives describing their day-to-day practice.
In this case, as in others, these stories are not the whole picture.

VIKI (see Figure 1a) is the technology that we ended up developing,
a workspace for gathering source documents and recording coarse-grained
interpretations of them. This example illustrates four requirements we
found central for the workspace. First, the workspace is an interpretive

infrastructure; it does not hold the documents. In this case, the documents themselves are Web pages and are simply referred to by URLs. This is not a radical idea given the way the Web implements URLs but, in pre-Web days, this kind of openness was considered an important—but not obvious—requirement.

The second aspect of the system is the ability to tailor a reduced representation of individual documents. In other words, each object in the interface represents a document and I, as a user, can dictate what form that should take—i.e., a title, an abstract, an automatic summary, and so on. Although this version of the system does not have the capacity, in

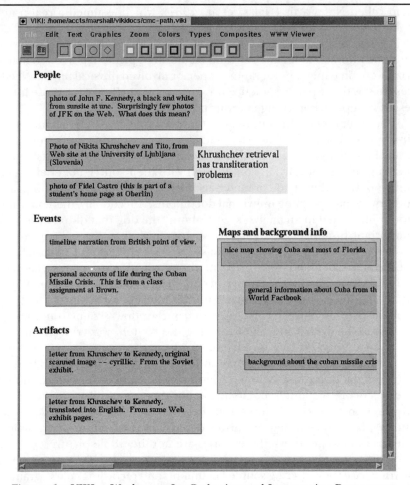

Figures 1a. VIKI, a Workspace for Gathering and Interpreting Documents.
Figure 1a Shows the Workspace Itself

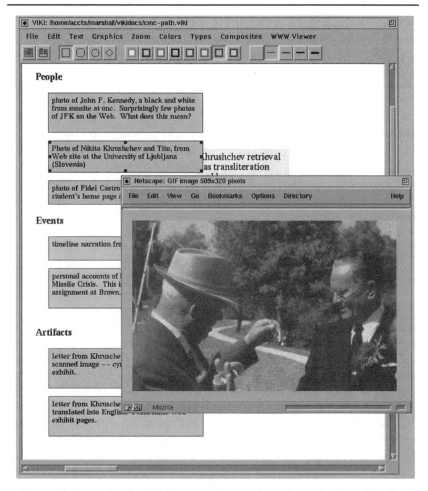

Figure 1b Example of a Web Browser that has been Launched as a Result of Clicking on a Visual Reference in Figure 1a

cases in which document types or genres are visually distinctive, a thumbnail is the ideal reduced representation.

Third, we use hierarchy to tame complexity. What we had in mind is a flexible means of either shifting from task to task, or task to subtask, while maintaining context. How is this realized? By providing subspaces so the main workspace can be subdivided. The references to individual documents can appear in as many subspaces as necessary.

The fourth aspect of this system that should be emphasized in this short account is manipulability and the ability to record ad hoc, partial, or ambiguous interpretations: it is what we most often lose when we go digital, and what I consider to be the truly annotative aspect of the system. I can change a document to red to signal to myself that it is important or that I need to come back to it, or that it is about Greece. It is these light-weight classifications that we need to reclaim in our digital library reading machines.

INFORMATION TRIAGE: AN EXPERIMENT

One important lesson we learned in this particular development effort is that work practices are dynamic, shifting with social changes. The study I described began before the fall of the Berlin Wall. By the time we had gone through a couple of different prototypes and had reached the system state illustrated by Figure 1, major changes had taken place in our users' work environment.

Although the analysts still performed long-term studies of technology, politics, or events in world regions, the institutional emphasis had shifted to shorter-term—oftentimes daily—results. Would our approach still make sense given this shift?

What we did to understand the effects of our technology on a very short-term analysis task is to conduct a controlled experiment, which was based on a real analysis.[2] Fifteen subjects were given a small corpus of relevant documents (seventy-five in all) and asked to perform an open-ended task over the course of forty-five minutes. The documents were the same set that had been collected from an information service for the real task and were incomplete, contradictory, and sometimes redundant. Some documents were frustratingly general; others were brief and highly specific. One-third of our subjects performed the analysis using paper; the second one-third used VIKI without the subspace mechanism; and the third group of subjects used a complete version of VIKI that allowed them to create and populate subspaces. Both versions of VIKI had a multi-term search capability that turned out to be very popular for winnowing down the document set to specific documents of interest.

Figure 2 shows what the space looked like at the outset. Each rectangle represents a single article. The title of the article is shown on the rectangle. The subjects using paper were given a comparable stack of print-outs of each article and appropriate office supplies like highlighters, pens, post-its, paper clips, and a stapler.[3]

Three results stood out: First, in many ways, the kinds of things people did to cope with the surfeit of relevant documents were remarkably similar. In all cases, people sorted the articles into rough categories; these categories shifted as they began to understand the nature of the corpus and the nature of the task. They had remarkably little patience for the general articles and discovered ways to get them "out of the way." Figure 3 shows a side-by-side comparison of two subjects' results. In Figure 3a, the categories are implemented as piles and "out of the way" meant on the floor. In Figure 3b, the categories are implemented as subspaces; documents deemed having little value for the analysis are left in their original positions. Second, the tool influenced the way people thought about the task. This variance is most evident in how they responded to the question, "What would you do if you had more time?" The subjects who completed the task using paper generally focused on reading; the subjects who tackled the analysis using the simplified version of VIKI without subspaces talked about organizing; and finally, the subjects who used the complete version of VIKI spoke even more intensely about their desire to create order. The following three responses to the "more time" question exemplify this effect:

> [I would] Read the info that I selected as critical more carefully and perhaps highlight some important text for my boss to help support my decision.—a subject from the paper condition.

> [I'd do a] better job of re-organizing the documents: I spent my time coming up with a recommendation, not organizing the documents.— a subject from the VIKI-without-subspaces condition.

> I would organize each big collection into smaller collections and possibly change some of the names. . . . Also I would look a little more carefully at some of the articles as some might be misplaced.— a subject from the VIKI-with-subspaces condition.

Finally, the question that lingered after the experiment was over was what would have happened if we had just allowed the subjects to do their own research on the Web? A well-constructed Boolean query that had been used to gather the source documents from an information service turned up 6,000 hits on the Web; sampling the hits showed many of them to be relevant. The type of information triage we investigated in our controlled experiment is bound to be a potential activity of digital library patrons when they find themselves gathering materials to answer open-ended questions.

K-12 TEACHERS AND STUDENTS MAKE THEIR WAY THROUGH THE WEB

The second story is one of annotation as a means of ordering "found" Web materials for presentation in a classroom setting. This story begins at the close of 1994 with a DARPA-sponsored project in the CAETI (Computer-Aided Education and Training Initiative) Program. What we set out to do in this project was to find a way to take advantage of what the Web can bring to the classroom in terms of access to information while still acknowledging that the Web is not a digital library—there are all kinds of materials on the Web that for one reason or another are over the kids'

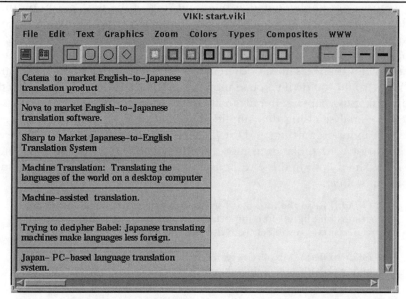

Figure 2. The Starting Out Configuration of the VIKI Workspace for the
Information Triage Experiment

Figures 3a. A Comparison of Two Subjects' Results from the Information
Triage Experiment. Figure 3a Shows a Subject Performing the Analysis Using
Paper Copies of the Article

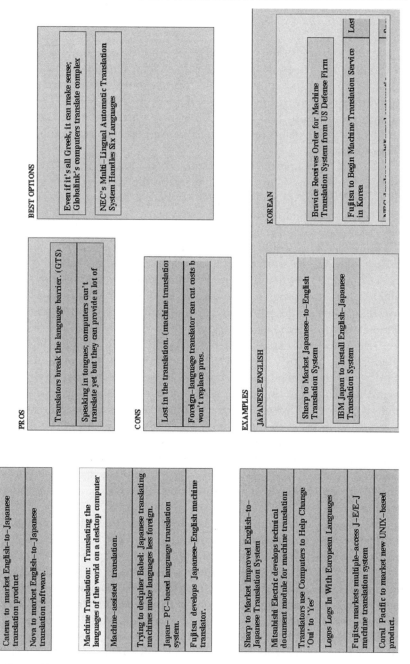

Figure 3b The Results of a Subject's Analysis of the Materials Using the VIKI
Workspace

heads or absolutely inappropriate for the classroom—and that the school setting introduces a variety of challenging technological and social constraints.

While we were in the early phases of our effort, we had the opportunity to observe classes of sixth graders from a local middle school using a standard browser to explore the Web. The sessions, which were part of a community enrichment program, took place in a Texas A & M engineering computer lab so that each student who participated in the session could sit in front of his or her own PC. We observed several important phenomena.

Paths were a natural way for students to approach the Web. If we listened to them, we heard things like, "How did you do that?" and "How did you get there?" Students helped each other navigate in a very literal sense: they would help another student retrace their own steps to get to a particular page on a Web site.

Some students would get stuck. They would reach a page that they did not expect to see or one that had no links out and instead of using the "back" button to retrace their steps (admittedly we all know this to be a fallible means of navigation, given the models of backtracking in Web browsers), they would simply give up and wait for help. Intervention was necessary to put them back on track.

The unfocused exploration, coupled with the fact that learning is an essentially social activity, proved to be interesting as well. It became apparent that the classes near the end of the day were affected by the discoveries of the students in the earlier sessions. During a morning session, one student discovered MTV's Beavis and Butthead site. Soon other students were following his path there, and apparently by the end of the day, students had figured out how to pass the URL to one another to navigate there directly. There are two conclusions we came to as a result of this observation: one is that learning has a certain collective quality to it, but more importantly, having a goal and guide to focus exploration is indeed necessary.

We developed a system called Walden's Paths to work in a K-12 classroom environment. The basic architecture of the system is constrained by existing technology, network bandwidth, and the exigencies of teaching and the classroom. Thus we designed the system as a proxy that would mediate between existing Web servers and clients so no new software needs to be purchased, and upgrades can be performed as needed. We also paid attention to caching strategies, since network bandwidth to classrooms is sometimes lower than need be. A path authoring tool allows teachers and students to assemble and annotate Web pages to form paths. The paths are linear in recognition of the time-consuming nature of developing a rhetorical structure for a nonlinear path.

Figures 4a and 4b show Web pages served by the path server. Note that the controls for moving along a path are readily available at the top of every page on the path. The arrows move a student forward or backward along the path; the numbers both show the number of stops that the tour has and allow the student to jump to a specific one. Below the controls are annotations added by the path author; in Figure 4a, the path author has added some material about Kennedy's victory in 1960 to a digital image gathered from the Web. Figure 4b illustrates the approach that Walden's Paths takes to student explorations "off-the-path." A control is added to take the student back to his or her jumping off point.

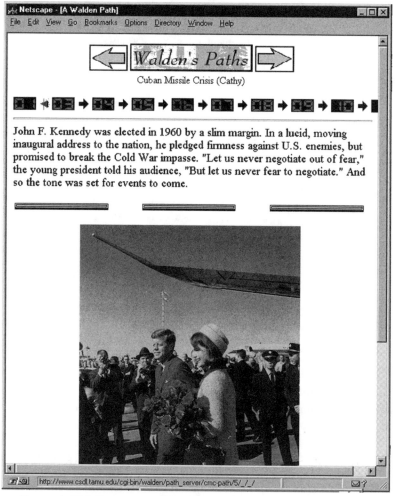

Figure 4a. Web Pages Served by the Walden's Paths Server. Figure 4a Shows a Page that is "On the Path"

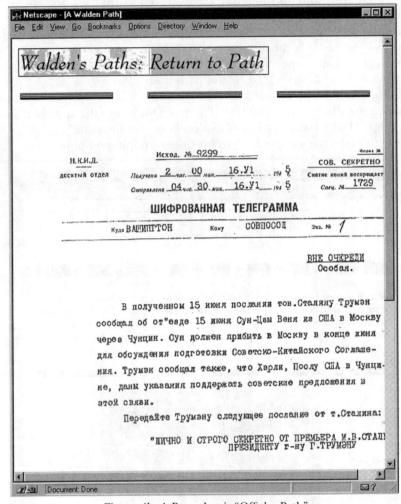

Figure 4b. A Page that is "Off the Path"

My colleagues Frank Shipman and Rick Furuta and their graduate students are continuing this work. The Walden's Path system has been used in classrooms for Department of Defense dependents in Germany and Italy (Shipman et al., 1998).

COLLEGE STUDENTS ENGAGED WITH THEIR TEXTS

The third story is about annotation as a reflection of students' engagement with their course textbooks. What I plan to do in this story is first to take a close look at annotation of individual texts to examine annotation as an individual practice, then move from there to suggest a movement toward an ecology of annotation.

Personal annotations in books have been the inspiration for hypertext systems builders (and hypertext advocates) for some time now, especially for those working in educational settings.[4] In his Hypertext '87 keynote address, Andreas van Dam (1988) spoke about the roots of his early hypertext system, FRESS:

> The reason I encouraged such annotations [in FRESS] was that I remembered that when I was in college with Ted [Nelson], I would always grab the dirtiest copy of a book from the library, rather than the cleanest one, because the dirtiest ones had the most marginalia, which I found helpful. (pp. 891-92)

If such an assumption is true—that annotations have value beyond the immediate—and that these annotations are created through a particular set of practices and activities, I began to wonder how annotation would take place in a digital library.

Some of these musings were simply about the marks themselves and the means of making them. As it stands, annotating digital materials is not a straightforward activity. We have neither the practices nor the tools for fluidly marking on digital materials in all the ways we mark on paper. Yet we often desire to do so. People print out documents to mark on them (O'Hara & Sellen, 1997).

Furthermore, as we all know as annotators ourselves, the functions of the markings people make as they read are not so simple. Yes, some of them are the kind of useful commentary van Dam is addressing, but other functions are evident from even the most casual look at annotations in action. So then, putting on my developer's hat, I felt obliged to ask, "How will the many functions of annotations inform implementation?"

Given that these annotations begin their life as a personal form and not as public commentary, we can move into the realm of the boundaries between private and public forms—boundaries that are often far more explicit and pronounced in the digital world than they are with paper documents. Will the move to digital materials make this seamless transition from a personal form to a public, often anonymous, form impossible? Coupled with this question is the very real question of whether a typical annotation has any lasting value relative to the potential permanence of the work itself. If it does not, then the transition between private and public is not particularly of interest to us.

Most generally then, I would like to pose the question: What does the activity of annotation on paper imply about reading and writing in the digital library? To help answer some of these questions, I used the crowded textbook section of a large university's bookstore as a source of both a community of annotators, and access to a large collection of annotated course materials. This bookstore, as well as many others, buys

back used textbooks no matter how heavily annotated they are as long as
the books' bindings and pages are intact. I've spent the first week or so
of classes in the bookstore over the course of four terms to get a good
sampling of both students and books.[5] To date, about 410 used books
were examined, representing thirty-nine titles (same edition) in twenty-
one general course areas. What the bookstore gives me is access to comparable copies of the same edition marked up under similar circumstances.

This setting, the university bookstore, has enabled me to not only
look at the annotations in the textbooks themselves but also to observe
the students choosing their books and talking among themselves about,
among other things, strategies for buying used books (Marshall, 1997). I
have also conducted open-ended informal interviews of textbook buyers,
often using the annotations of other students to provoke comments and
reactions, and to help students describe their own annotation practices.
Most recently, I have performed a detailed comparison of copies of a single
edition to better understand how annotations made by many different
members of a community add up (Marshall, 1998).

The form of these markings is, as one would expect, incredibly fluid.
Annotations are made using all manner and all colors of specialized mark-
ers, pens, pencils, and—most generally—anything that can leave a record
on paper. Likewise, any markable area of a book might have annotations
on it.

But what is more interesting is that there are some notable strategies
people bring to bear in their annotations. First, most often annotators use
the writing implement that is "at hand." Evidence for this is in the correlation between penned marginalia and underlining; I also found notes written in highlighter (an awkward writing implement at best—these notes
are usually quite short). Second, there were a small number of complex
(but implicit) coding schemes that annotators had developed. The fact
that the number was small is probably of greater interest than that they
existed at all; it is a great temptation to propose schemes for digital tools
in which pen color means something and is used computationally in some
way. It was rare to find one of these schemes that lasted throughout a
textbook. Finally, it seems that form follows textbook genre and expected
disciplinary practices. This observation should come as no surprise since
works in different disciplines are "read" differently.[6]

An example of a technology that might be a good basis for Patrick
Bazin's digital library reading machine has been developed at Fuji Xerox's
Palo Alto Laboratory. It is called XLibris (Schilit et al., 1998) and features
a pen-based interface, a portrait page orientation, and is about the size of
a laptop computer. This device is document-centered, rather than appli-
cation-centered, and supports the fluid kinds of markings encountered in
paper books.

The function of these annotations appears to vary a great deal, from clearly interpretive—marginalia that adds to the source text, as in Figure 5, part A—to asterisks that signal importance—but not why the passage is important, as in figure 5, part B—to page after page of highlighted text, as if the reader is marking his or her attendance to difficult or particularly dense writing, as in Figure 6. From an implementor's point of view, it is clear that at least some of these markings should be considered as transient evidence of a reader's engagement with the text.

What is more at issue here than the form annotations take and the functions they serve is their ultimate value. As you might guess, observations bear out all intuitions that some of these annotations are valuable and others merely annoying. Some students looked for books that were as pristine as a used book ever is, and others took up strategies like the one I heard discussed,"Look for writing in the margins and no highlighting. Sentences not just phrases." There was clear evidence that some found all annotations distracting, and other students tolerated some kinds of writing—e.g., yellow highlighter—more than others—e.g., black ballpoint underlines.

It is also clear that whatever we conceive of doing with these annotations in a digital world, we must take strict account of the fact that they are a private form of writing, made public only through assumptions of anonymity. Expectations of privacy manifested themselves in telling ways: stray signed credit card slips tucked in between the pages and names and social security numbers written inside front covers.

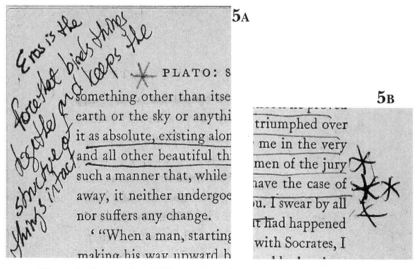

Figure 5. Contrasting Different Functions of Annotations. 5A is an Interpretation Written in the Margins; 5B indicates Emphasis Markings

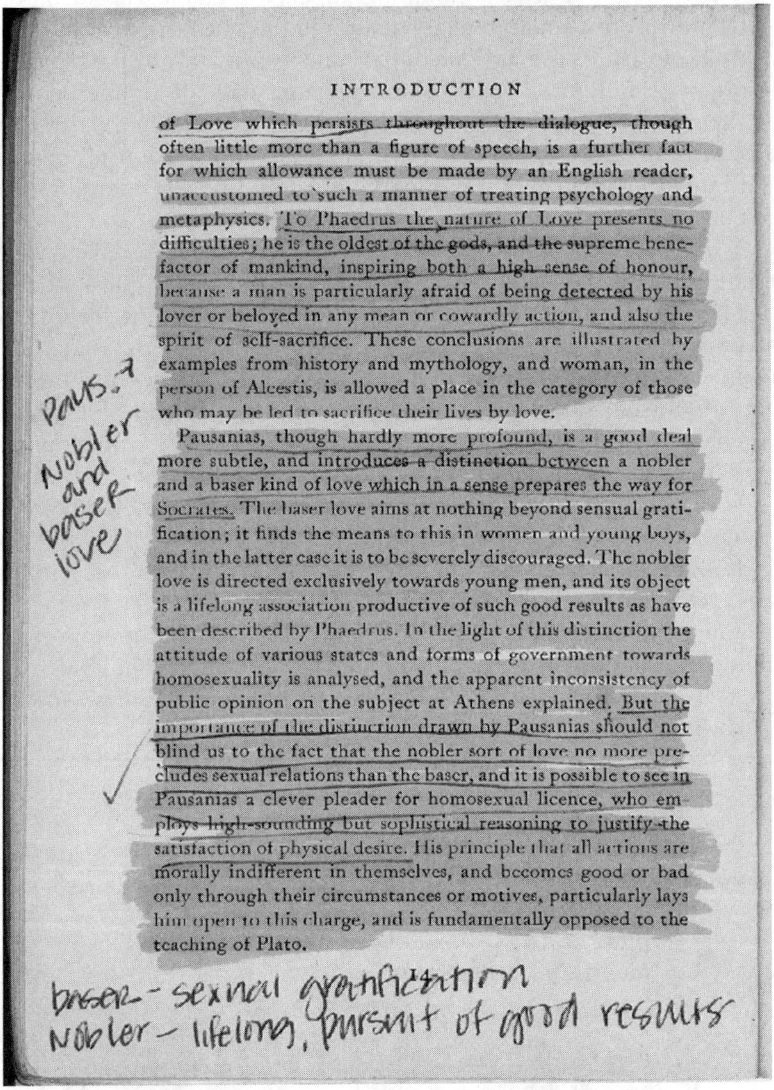

INTRODUCTION

of Love which persists throughout the dialogue, though often little more than a figure of speech, is a further fact for which allowance must be made by an English reader, unaccustomed to such a manner of treating psychology and metaphysics. To Phaedrus the nature of Love presents no difficulties; he is the oldest of the gods, and the supreme benefactor of mankind, inspiring both a high sense of honour, because a man is particularly afraid of being detected by his lover or beloved in any mean or cowardly action, and also the spirit of self-sacrifice. These conclusions are illustrated by examples from history and mythology, and woman, in the person of Alcestis, is allowed a place in the category of those who may be led to sacrifice their lives by love.

Pausanias, though hardly more profound, is a good deal more subtle, and introduces a distinction between a nobler and a baser kind of love which in a sense prepares the way for Socrates. The baser love aims at nothing beyond sensual gratification; it finds the means to this in women and young boys, and in the latter case it is to be severely discouraged. The nobler love is directed exclusively towards young men, and its object is a lifelong association productive of such good results as have been described by Phaedrus. In the light of this distinction the attitude of various states and forms of government towards homosexuality is analysed, and the apparent inconsistency of public opinion on the subject at Athens explained. But the importance of the distinction drawn by Pausanias should not blind us to the fact that the nobler sort of love no more precludes sexual relations than the baser, and it is possible to see in Pausanias a clever pleader for homosexual licence, who employs high-sounding but sophistical reasoning to justify the satisfaction of physical desire. His principle that all actions are morally indifferent in themselves, and becomes good or bad only through their circumstances or motives, particularly lays him open to this charge, and is fundamentally opposed to the teaching of Plato.

[Handwritten marginal notes: "Paus.? nobler and baser love"]

[Handwritten notes below figure: "baser - sexual gratification / nobler - lifelong, pursuit of good results"]

Figure 6. Example of Dense Noninterpretive Highlighting

Taking privacy into account, and considering the kinds of marks that were the most common throughout the textbook sample—highlights and emphasis marks like stars and asterisks—I tried to imagine what sorts of things one could do with these annotations in a digital library environment. This environment might be a place in which one could computationally harvest transient annotations (given a reading machine) in a wholly anonymous and transparent way. What sort of consensus do readers reach? How can it be used in ways that respect both a reader's sense of order and an author's sense of the original structure of the work?

To answer this question for myself, a study was performed (Marshall, 1998) in which I did a sentence-by-sentence analysis of seven copies of a particular textbook—a computer science textbook in which the presentation was in a narrative form. The results, although preliminary, were convincing. Readers achieve some level of consensus about where the key passages are in each chapter of the book. These passages are not necessarily the rhetorically predictable ones (i.e., the topic sentences at the beginning of sections or even the topic sentences of paragraphs) but rather occur in the midst of loci of annotative activity and do have some significance.

WHERE TO NEXT?

What might we do if we took the desire for a digital library reading machine seriously? First, there are some serious questions to answer about how and where marking should take place. If it is to take place digitally, how can we truly capture the fluidity of form we see on paper? Should we posit a digital library reading machine that is stylus-driven and document-centered like the XLibris device?

Given the right device for personal annotation, we have only answered part of the question. Annotation spans a huge range of activities, activities that may include proofreading and writing commentary to an audience. Can all these forms of annotative activity be supported by a single type of reading machine? Can they be subsumed by a general architecture? Phelps and Wilensky's (1997) work on multivalent documents as the basis for layering on annotations begins to investigate some of these questions. The older ComMentor facility at Stanford, which was based on the NCSA Mosaic annotation function, also assumed that indeed a single general architecture for annotation is an appropriate goal (Roescheisen et al., 1994).

From the results at the bookstore, it looks like it is important for the reading machine to support noninterpretive marking as well as interpretive markings. Given that one might feed into a consensus mechanism like the one I have been discussing, and the other is probably not useful beyond the current reading, is there a way to tell the difference between the two?

And what of interpretive markings? Can we in some way assess their value and intelligibility? How do they function as shared forms? Their intelligibility is always at stake, yet it is clear that sharing interpretive annotations is one of the benefits of working in a mixed digital-physical environment in which at least some document surrogate exists online.

Finally, and most essentially, how can we move toward smooth integration of annotation with the various kinds of reading (intensive, extensive, hyperextensive) we see today? In an intensive reading situation, annotation must represent a deep unself-conscious engagement with the text. In an extensive reading situation, documents or their surrogates must be readily manipulable and easy to juxtapose or informally link. In a hyperextensive reading situation, annotation can and should be a means of easing the fragmentation.

Finally, considering annotation in the large, how can we support the seamless kinds of transitions between private and anonymous public annotations that we see in the bookstore? How can they be used collectively to form an ecology as we begin to understand their status and value? Most importantly, how can we encourage the establishment and growth of these ecologies without ignoring questions of scope and community?

The development of the reading machine of tomorrow, one that acknowledges the depth and variability of the reader's engagement with the texts in a mixed digital-physical library, is indeed a tall order.

NOTES

[1] This article describes three very different communities which might take advantage of new digital resources, including short accounts of technologies I and others have developed to support their activities as they use formal collections and more ad hoc resources. In fact, what I hope to do is to advocate annotation as a key function to what Patrick Bazin (1996) refers to as a reading machine. But first, I'd like to clarify what I mean when I say "annotation."

[2] A complete account of the experiment and its results is presented in Marshall and Shipman (1997).

[3] In some ways, the reduced document representation that VIKI showed, the titles, was not entirely comparable to the paper condition, in which subjects always saw the entire first page of the document.

[4] See, for example, Landow's (1992) essay. Such annotations have also stirred considerable interest in the community of people developing computational support for online technical manuals and the like.

[5] In particular, since annotation is a learned practice, incoming freshmen and their used texts are quite different from upperclassmen and their used texts.

[6] For example, heavy use of a yellow highlighter in the first few chapters of a math textbook does not bode well for the student; by convention, math textbooks begin with review, and memorization is usually less important than the ability to reason with and from the material.

REFERENCES

Bazin, P. (1996). Toward metareading. In G. Nunberg (Ed.), *The future of the book* (pp. 153-168). Berkeley: University of California Press.

Bush, V. (1945). As we may think. *Atlantic Monthly*, (August), 101-108.

Furuta, R.; Shipman, F. M., III; Marshall, C. C.; Brenner, D.; & Hsieh, H. (1997). Hypertext paths and the World-Wide Web: Experiences with Walden's Paths. In *Proceedings of Hypertext '97* (pp. 167-176). New York: ACM Press.

Grudin, J. (1989). The case against user interface consistency. *Communications of the ACM, 32*(10), 1164-1173.

Halasz, F. G.; Moran, T. P.; & Trigg, R. H. (1987). NoteCards in a nutshell. In *Proceedings of the ACM CHI + GI Conference* (pp. 45-52). New York: ACM Press.

Landow, G. P. (1992). *Hypertext: The convergence of contemporary critical theory and technology.* Baltimore, MD: Johns Hopkins University Press.

Levy, D. M. (1995). Cataloging in the digital order. In *Proceedings of Digital Libraries '95* (pp. 31-37). College Station: Texas A & M University, Center for the Study of Digital Libraries.

Levy, D. M. (1997). I read the news today oh boy: Reading and attention in the digital library. In *Proceedings of Digital Libraries '97* (pp. 202-211). New York: ACM.

Marshall, C. C. (1990). *Work practice study: Analysts and notetaking.* Unpublished Technical Report, Xerox Palo Alto Research Center.

Marshall, C. C. (1997). Annotation: From paper books to the digital library. In *Proceedings of Digital Libraries '97* (pp. 131-140). New York: ACM.

Marshall, C. C. (1998). Toward an ecology of hypertext annotation. To appear in *Proceedings of Hypertext '98.* New York: ACM.

Marshall, C. C., & Shipman, F. M., III. (1995). Spatial hypertext: Designing for change. *Communications of the ACM, 38*(8), 88-97.

Marshall, C. C., & Shipman, F. M., III. (1997). Spatial hypertext and the practice of information triage. In *Proceedings of Hypertext '97* (pp. 124-133). New York: ACM.

McCrum, R. (1994). A life in the margins. *New Yorker,* April 11, 46-55.

Moulthrop, S. (1993). You say you want a revolution: Hypertext and the laws of media. In E. Amiran & J. Unsworth (Eds.), *Essays in postmodern culture* (pp. 69-97). New York: Oxford University Press.

O'Hara, K., & Sellen, A. (1997). A comparison of reading paper and on-line documents. In *Proceedings of CHI '97* (pp. 335-342). New York: ACM.

Phelps, T. A., & Wilensky, R. (1997). *Multivalent annotations.* Unpublished paper presented at the Proceedings of the First European Conference on Research and Advanced Technology for Digital Libraries, 1-3 September 1997, Pisa, Italy.

Roescheisen, M.; Mogensen, C.; & Winograd, T. (1994). *Shared Web annotations as a platform for third-party value-added information providers: Architecture, protocols, and usage examples.* Unpublished Technical Report STAN-CS-TR-97-1582, Stanford Integrated Digital Library Project, Computer Science Dept., Stanford University. November 1994, updated April 1995.

Schilit, B.; Price, M.; & Golovchinsky, G. (1998). The digital library information appliance. In *Proceedings of ACM Digital Libraries '98.* New York: ACM Press.

Shipman, F. M., III; Furuta, R.; Brenner, D.; Chung, C.; & Hsieh, H. (1998). Using paths in the classroom: Experiences and adaptations. To appear in *Proceedings of Hypertext '98.* New York: ACM Press.

van Dam, A. (1988). Hypertext '87 keynote address. *Communications of the ACM, 31*(7), 887-895.

GIVE ME DOCUMENTS OR GIVE ME DEATH

A MILLENNIAL MEDITATION ON DOCUMENTS AND LIBRARIES

David M. Levy

INTRODUCTION

Who can doubt that these are exciting times, pregnant with possibility? Current technological developments, such as the World Wide Web, seem to promise new and more engaging ways of learning, access to great storehouses of knowledge, and breakthroughs in science and scholarship. Yet at the same time, it is hard not to notice the undercurrent of anxiety that accompanies the current excitement. Many are confused about the changes now underway, unclear about how broad or deep they will be, and how exactly they will affect us. What will happen to the library, to the book, to publishing as we now know it, to education? These can seem like big abstract questions, but they have a highly personal component. For what is also being asked is, what does all this mean for me—for my livelihood, my family, my children, for my sense of order, well-being, and meaning?

What is happening, I believe, is that current technological and institutional changes are challenging our sense of order—our sense of living in a carefully regulated, secure, and ultimately meaningful universe. When this sense of order is challenged, we become anxious. Why? The answer seems obvious enough. When our world becomes unstable, we worry about losing our jobs, our professional standing, our income, and all the physical, psychological, and social comforts that come with these. While this is clear enough, there may also be a deeper source for the current anxiety—an existential source—which underlies all the very real concerns about livelihood and status: namely, the fear of death. On the face of it, death hardly seems like a fitting subject for a workshop sponsored by the Graduate School of Library and Information Science. What does death have to do with digital libraries? A great deal, as I hope to show, for documents are intimately and essentially concerned with making order in the world, and order-making is a response to the fact of death.

THE ANXIETY OF ORDER

As a starting point, the problem of order and disorder will be considered. Documents and libraries, of course, have a great deal to do with order. Libraries are concerned with bringing order to documents and collections of documents. Cataloging, conservation and preservation, reference services, and so on are all about keeping written materials orderly and allowing them to be found and used in an orderly manner. Without such carefully worked out practices, we would have disorder—a lack of order. The current state of the Web—the transience of the materials on it, the difficulty of finding anything, and of knowing what you've got once you've found it—has provided many people, technologists not the least of them, with an important lesson. Many of us have used libraries without ever understanding the extent of the invisible work that was being done day by day to ensure that books stayed on shelves and in proper states of repair. If the current state of the Web has taught us anything, it is how crucial is the ever ongoing invisible work of order-making (Levy, 1995).

Roger Chartier (1994) provides a useful historical perspective on these practices when he observes that a tremendous amount of work was required, after the invention of the printing press, to "set the world of the written word in order":

> [H]ow did people in Western Europe between the end of the Middle Ages and the eighteenth century attempt to master the enormously increased number of texts that first the manuscript book and then print put into circulation? Inventorying titles, categorizing works, and attributing texts were all operations that made it possible to set the world of the written word in order. Our own age is the direct heir of this immense effort motivated by anxiety. (p. vii)

Implicitly, Chartier seems to be suggesting that we are now on the verge of another "immense effort motivated by anxiety." But why anxiety?

Anxiety, it seems to me, is always associated with order. There is, in effect, an anxiety of order. It is an obvious enough truism that human beings crave order: we want or need to control our environment. On a purely biological level, we need to guarantee a steady supply of food and water, protection from the elements, and so on. For social well-being, we need to keep our emotions within acceptable limits, and we need to work out orderly "civilized" practices with one another. This is fundamentally an issue of survival. Without enough of just the right stuff, we will die. Social ostracism, although not necessarily biologically fatal, is surely also a form of death—a social or symbolic death. If order-making is at base an attempt to stay alive, to stave off death, then it makes sense that there would be anxiety associated with it, if only unconsciously.

Order-making, of course, only goes so far as a survival strategy. The truth is that no matter how well we order things, no matter how much successful control we exert, we will still ultimately die. It is left to each of us to come to terms with this ultimate existential fact. The cultural anthropologist Ernest Becker has suggested that all human culture is essentially a response to the fact of death. In his Pulitzer Prize-winning book, *The Denial of Death*, Becker (1973) suggests that human culture is the attempt to create something larger and enduring—something we can be part of and through which we can live on—in the hope of achieving a kind of greatness or immortality. It is a system, he says:

> in which people serve in order to earn a feeling of primary value, of cosmic specialness, of ultimate usefulness to creation, of unshakable meaning. They earn this feeling by carving out a place in nature, by building an edifice that reflects human value: a temple, a cathedral, a totem pole, a sky-scraper, a family that spans three generations. The hope and belief is that the things that man creates in society are of lasting worth and meaning, that they outlive or outshine death and decay, that man and his products count. (p. 4)

If, as Becker suggests, culture is our collective attempt to deny and to transcend death, then it makes sense that all cultural order-making practices would have—if only at an unconscious level—a degree of anxiety associated with them. It makes sense that we would become anxious when the carefully worked out and maintained cultural order breaks down, or when it becomes transparent enough to allow us to see what lies just beyond it. These breakdowns would act as a reminder that disarray and disorder—and, ultimately, death—are never really that far from us.

A few years ago, I was shocked when I walked into the Saks Fifth Avenue in the Stanford Shopping Center. Instead of finding the brightly lit glittery store with aisles full of expensive merchandise beautifully displayed—the shop I'd been in many times before—I found a dingy run-down excuse for a store. Paint was peeling off the walls, display counters were nicked and tattered, and the merchandise was in disarray; it had a slightly used air about it. I walked outside, just to make sure I had found the right building, but also to clear my head from the shock and confusion. As I re-entered the building, I noticed a sign I hadn't seen when I entered the store the first time. It explained that Saks was closing and the building was being used as a "seconds" store for Saks merchandise. What I had obviously encountered was a store in decline. Through their elaborate and highly tuned order (lighting, display, music, and so on), fancy department stores like Saks try to suggest a timeless and perfect order, an effortless happiness, which can be ours if we will only buy the right things. We are never meant to see the huge amount of work that is required to maintain the illusion. What I had seen was the inevitable decline that occurs when the invisible ever-ongoing work of maintaining the order is withheld. And what I experienced was not just the shock of the unexpected but a confrontation with the chaos that lies just behind the carefully maintained façade. It was a reminder that all our structures, ultimately, are transient and impermanent.

Libraries are like this too. A huge amount of work has gone into the development of their various order-making systems—cataloging and reference services, preservation, and so on. For most of our lifetime, they have been symbols of rationality and order. But now, as I noted earlier, it is becoming increasingly clear how much invisible work has been required to maintain that illusion. And it is clear that we don't yet know how to adapt this invisible work to handle the new materials and the new technologies. Of course it isn't just libraries that are part of the cultural ordering system. So too are the construction industry, the garbage collection industry, the fashion industry, the media. Indeed, if Becker is right, all of human social and cultural life is part of this ordering system. Still, there is something special about libraries which makes disruption to them an even greater source of anxiety. Libraries are keepers of documents, and documents have a crucial role to play in establishing and maintaining order.

DOCUMENTS AND ORDER

By documents, I mean written forms, broadly construed. The category of documents includes textual materials on paper (job applications and newspapers, cash register receipts and books, shopping lists and magazines), graphical forms of all kinds (maps and photographs, drawings and diagrams), and "written" forms realized in other media (digital spreadsheets and Web pages, audiotapes and videotapes). What all these have in common is that, in one fashion or another, they fix or stabilize communication—they hold it fixed or make it repeatable so that the same words (or sounds or images) can be seen by people separated in space and time. This ability to hold communication fixed provides one of the central building blocks out of which all our major cultural institutions are constructed and maintained. Science, law and government, religion, education, and the arts all rely on the stabilizing power of documents to help maintain their own stability. Thus, in the form of books and journal articles, documents are carriers of scientific knowledge. As sacred scripture, they are the central artifacts around which religious traditions have been organized. As written statutes, charters, and contracts, they play a crucial role in constructing and regulating lawful behavior. As works of literature, paintings, and drawings, they are the tangible products of artistic practice. As textbooks and student notes, they are crucial instruments around which learning practices are organized.

These institutions are themselves central players in the construction of an ongoing meaningful daily order. Science and religion, in quite different ways, seek to identify and explain the underlying orderliness of the universe. Law and government provide a regulatory framework. Education has a "civilizing" function. The arts are means by which we represent (and some would say, construct) a meaningful universe. By supporting these institutions, documents thereby play a crucial role in supporting the ongoing order.

But it is a mistake to think that documents are somehow "naturally" stable or orderly. Just as a Saks Fifth Avenue will decay and disappear without constant maintenance, the same will happen to individual documents or collections unless they are constantly tended. And so we have a secondary set of institutions—including libraries, archives, publishers, copyright, and the courts—which work to stabilize documents so they can in turn support and stabilize science, education, and so on.

Until quite recently, these order-making practices—both the use of documents to stabilize institutions and the use of institutions to stabilize documents—were based on paper, print, and the various genres of documents which have arisen from these technologies. But now, the emergence of digital technologies and digital document forms has introduced great uncertainty into most, if not all, of these institutions. Many questions cannot yet be answered. How must current institutional practices be modified to accommodate these new forms? How will we stabilize and preserve them? It seems that the whole order-making system, our cover for death, is reeling. The cracks are showing like the deteriorating walls and counters in Saks Fifth Avenue. Is it any wonder we are anxious?

What I've just suggested, then, is that documents and institutions are mutually stabilizing. The same can be said about documents and selves or documents and individuals. Sherry Turkle (1984) has suggested that computers are "second selves"—devices onto which we project aspects of our persona or inner being. Documents can be understood in this way, too. They too are second selves which work to stabilize us as we work to stabilize them. To see this, it is useful to notice that documents are essentially talking things. They are bits of the material world—clay, stone, animal skin, plant fiber, sand—that we've imbued with the ability to speak. One of the earliest characterizations of documents comes from Genesis, the first book of the Judeo-Christian Bible and, curiously, it is a description of human beings, not of written forms: "God formed Adam from the dust of the earth, and blew into his nostrils the breath of life, and Adam became a living soul." The parallel between this mythic event and the creation of actual documents is strikingly close. For indeed, what we do when we make documents is to take the dust of the earth and breathe our breath, our voice, into it.

Framing documents in this way sets up a strong parallel between documents and people. Each in their own way are talking things. This is hardly an accidental parallel. Documents are exactly those things we create to speak for us—on our behalf and in our absence. And in speaking for us, they take on work, they do jobs for us. They are surrogate selves. Each genre—each kind of document—is the encapsulation of some part of ourselves, some manner of operating or being in the world. This is obviously the case for a love letter, a personal journal entry, or an office memo, but it is equally true for a bank statement, a road sign, or a restaurant menu (although in these latter cases the self being represented may be an institutional or organizational self). We have in effect constructed documents in our own image, and they resemble us, not only functionally, insofar as they speak and work for us, but structurally too. Documents, like human beings, have a material component and a symbolic component—in effect, a body and a soul. For millennia, human beings have hoped and believed that some part of themselves was immortal, that this part (call it the soul) lived on and transcended the death of the body. But at the same time, people have used documents as a way to transcend death—as a way to transfer some part of themselves into another body. Indeed, since ancient times, the written word has been seen as a way to cheat death. The hope has been—for certain authors at least, the so-called Immortals—that one could live on through one's works, that one could transcend the limits of bodily existence. The hope has been to live on through these surrogates, these second selves, much as we might hope to live on through our children.

Paper documents are fairly reassuring as second selves. They are whole, they have clear boundaries and healthy bodies and, under the right conditions, they can last for hundreds of years. It is not so with digital documents—at least as they exist today, they are pieced together from hyperlinked fragments; they seem to be abandoning their bodies (becoming virtual); and they are highly transient or impermanent. Breaking into pieces, giving up one's body, and being impermanent—what does this suggest if not death and dying? It hardly seems surprising that second selves displaying such properties would be a cause for anxiety.

KNOWLEDGE AND LIBRARIES

As another way to examine the anxiety of the times, I next want to consider how libraries participate in the quest for knowledge. The library has long symbolized the quest for knowledge. Practically speaking, libraries have been storehouses or treasure chests for the preservation of human knowledge. But beyond this, they have held out, at least in imagination, the hope of collecting all knowledge in one place and thus creating a universal library. In his story, "The Library of Babel," collected in *Laby-*

rinths, Jorges Luis Borges (1964) plays on this theme, imagining a universe which is a library: "The universe (which others call the library) is composed of an indefinite, and perhaps infinite, number of hexagonal galleries, with vast air shafts between, surrounded by very low railings." In an essay entitled "Libraries without Walls" collected in his book, *The Order of Books,* Chartier (1994) begins by quoting from this same story: "When it was proclaimed that the Library contained all books, the first impression was one of extravagant happiness." He then goes on to say:

> The dream of a library (in a variety of configurations) that would bring together all accumulated knowledge and all the books ever written can be found throughout the history of Western civilization. It underlay the constitution of great princely, ecclesiastical, and private "libraries"; it justified a tenacious search for rare books, lost editions, and texts that had disappeared; it commanded architectural projects to construct edifices capable of welcoming the world's memory. (p. 62)

And in the epilogue to his book, he suggests that the dream of a universal library may finally be within our grasp:

> As the twentieth century wanes, our dream is to be able to surmount the contradiction that long haunted Western Europeans' relationship with the book. . . . The opposition long held to be insurmountable between the closed world of any finite collection, no matter what its size, and the infinite universe of all texts ever written is thus theoretically annihilated: now the catalogue of all catalogues ideally listing the totality of written production can be realized in a universal access to texts available for consultation at the reader's location. (pp. 89-90)

Whether or not a true universal library will ever be possible, it is clear that the longing for it is real enough. We long to know more, to acquire more knowledge about ourselves and the world, to store it, cross-reference it, and use it to our best advantage. Indeed, as far as we can tell, we are the only beings capable of knowing in these ways. But to know—to be capable of thinking and knowing—is both a blessing and a curse. It is a blessing in virtue of the experiences and the power it makes available to us—the joy of learning and discovery; the pleasures and insights of art; the control of our world and ourselves which science and technology afford. But it is also a curse insofar as it permits us to know one very specific existential fact—the fact of our impermanence, our mortality. Our condition, says Becker, is an existential paradox:

> The essence of man is his paradoxical nature, the fact that he is half animal and half symbolic. . . . We might call this existential paradox the condition of individuality within finitude. Man has a symbolic identity that brings him sharply out of nature. He is a symbolic self, a creature with a name, a life history. He is a creator with a mind that soars out to speculate about atoms and infinity, who can place himself

imaginatively at a point in space and contemplate bemusedly his own planet. This immense expansion, this dexterity, this ethereality, this self-consciousness gives to man literally the status of a small god in nature, as the Renaissance thinkers knew. (p. 26)

But we are mortal gods. And just as our capacity to know permits us—indeed forces us—to recognize our limited existence, it also gives us the capacity to respond to it. What is the striving to know more if not a response to the ultimate existential fact, an attempt to know our fate, and perhaps to change it? Isn't science ultimately concerned with trying to fathom the nature of the universe into which we've so mysteriously emerged? And isn't it also concerned—through medicine and genetic engineering—with helping us to extend our lives and perhaps (who knows?) to reverse the death sentence which comes with our animal nature?

What I have been suggesting, then, is that the quest for knowledge, if followed back to its existential roots, ultimately leads us to the question of human existence and the fact of death. Anxiety therefore underlies knowing and the quest for knowledge, just as it underlies our order-making activities. Whether we think of libraries as collections of documents or storehouses of knowledge, we come to the same conclusion: libraries and death are intimately related.

CONCLUSION

The point of these reflections has not been to suggest practical next steps in the design of technology or in the rethinking of institutional practices. Rather, my concern has been to locate the changes now taking place in a larger landscape—one might even say in a cosmic landscape. What could be bigger than questions of life and death? It is important for us to realize, as we pursue our powerful technologically dominated agenda, that we are not simply managing bits and bytes. Nor are we simply creating new institutional possibilities (as important as this may be). Instead, we are actually touching the soft and vulnerable core of who we humans are, how we know ourselves, and what we take ourselves to be. We must proceed with great care.

But ultimately, why talk about a subject as discomfiting, as potentially depressing, as death? Surely not to spoil the party. To talk about death is also and inevitably to make reference to life, whether implicitly or explicitly. Surely the most authentic response to the human condition—to the mystery of our existence, to the fact of our mortality—is to live more fully. What this might mean is left to each of us to discover. At a workshop whose topic is "successes and failures of digital libraries," I have simply wanted to propose a criterion—perhaps the ultimate existential criterion—by which to judge success and failure. I have simply wanted to raise this question: To what extent and in what ways can the current technological developments help us to live richer, fuller, and more meaningful lives?

In the early 1980s, after finishing graduate work in computer science, I went to London to study calligraphy. Until the invention of the printing press, and for some period afterward, calligraphy—writing with the broad edged pen—was the craft by which all manuscripts and books were produced. But as the printing press came to dominate book production, calligraphy gradually fell into disuse and, by the beginning of this century, the craft had essentially been lost. It was recovered in the early part of the century, thanks to the efforts of one man, an Englishman named Edward Johnston, who spent years pouring over manuscripts in the British Museum, gradually rediscovering how the technology of the broad-edged pen actually worked. I mention this only to introduce the quote with which I want to close. "Our aim must be," said Johnston, "to make letters live, so that we may have more life." If we hold this as our highest objective, then I am sure our technological efforts will be successful, and we will come to know "extravagant happiness."

REFERENCES

Becker, E. (1973). *The denial of death.* New York: The Free Press.

Borges, J. L. (1964). *Labyrinths.* New York: New Directions.

Chartier, R. (1994). *The order of books.* Stanford, CA: Stanford University Press.

Levy, D.M. (1995) Cataloging in the digital order. In F. M. Shipman III, R. Furuta, & D. M. Levy (Eds.), *Proceedings of Digital Libraries '95* (the second annual conference on the theory and practice of digital libraries, Austin, TX, June 11-13, 1995) (pp. 31-37). College Station, TX: Hypermedia Research Laboratory, Texas A&M University. Retrieved January 21, 2000 from the World Wide Web: http://csdl.tamu.edu/DL95/papers/levy/levy.html.

Turkle, S. (1984). *The second self: Computers and the human spirit.* New York: Simon and Schuster.

CONTRIBUTORS

ANN PETERSON BISHOP is an Assistant Professor in the Graduate School of Library and Information Science at the University of Illinois at Urbana-Champaign. Her primary research interest is social aspects of information system design, evaluation, and use. Most recently, she has pursued this interest in relation to digital libraries and community-based computer networks. Dr. Bishop has recently published (in the Proceedings of Digital Libraries 98) a paper on how researchers use individual components of journal articles. She is currently undertaking a study (funded by the U.S. Department of Commerce and the Kellogg Foundation) of the introduction of computers in low-income neighborhoods and its relationship to community information exchange and problem-solving.

HSINCHUN CHEN is McClelland Endowed Professor of MIS at the University of Arizona and Andersen Consulting Professor of the Year. He serves on the editorial board of the *Journal of the American Society for Information Science* and *Decision Support Systems*. He is an expert in digital library and knowledge management research, whose work has been featured in various scientific and information technologies publications including *Science*, *Business Week*, *NCSA Access Magazine*, *WEBster*, and *HCPWire*.

TIMOTHY W. COLE is currently an Assistant Engineering Librarian for Information Services and Associate Professor of Library Automation at the Grainger Agricultural Library at the University of Illinois at Urbana-Champaign.

EDWARD A. FOX is Professor in the Department of Computer Science, Associate Director for Research at the Computing Center, and Director of the Digital Library Research Laboratory at Virginia Tech in Blacksburg,

Virginia. He has written over 150 publications and, in addition, given over 150 presentations dealing with digital libraries, information retrieval, multimedia, electronic publishing, educational innovation, and other topics. He is editor for the Morgan Kaufmann book series on Multimedia Information and Systems, a member of seven editorial boards, and director of the Networked Digital Library of Theses and Dissertations.

STEPHEN M. GRIFFIN is a Program Director in the Division of Information, and Intelligent Systems at the National Science Foundation (NSF). He is currently Program Director for Special Projects and for the Interagency Digital Libraries Initiative. Prior to his current assignment, Mr. Griffin served in several research divisions, including the Divisions of Chemistry and Advanced Scientific Computing, the Office of the Assistant Director, Directorate for Computer and Information Science and Engineering, and staff offices of the Director of the NSF. He has been active in working groups of the Federal High Performance Computing and Communications Program. His educational background includes degrees in Chemical Engineering and Information Systems Technology. He has additional graduate education in organizational behavior and development and the philosophy of science. His research interests are in topics related to interdisciplinary communication.

SUSAN HARUM is External Relations Coordinator for the Digital Libraries Initiative at the Grainger Library at the University of Illinois at Urbana-Champaign.

THOMAS HICKEY is Chief Scientist, Office of Research, Online Computer Library Center (OCLC) in Dublin, Ohio. He started research into digital publication of scholarly journals in the early 1980s developing systems including Guidon, OCLC's first interface for such journals. In addition to research in various areas of library and information science, he co-designed and wrote the first version of the OCLC FirstSearch system and developed and lead the current CORC internet cataloging project through its first year.

TIM INGOLDSBY is Director of Business Development for the American Institute of Physics (AIP). He is responsible for AIP's interactions with other publishers and service providers and a frequent speaker at industry conferences dealing with the issues of the digital publishing era. He was recently named chair of the Publications Track for the Council of Engineering and Scientific Society Executives.

ERIC H. JOHNSON is a member of the CANIS Community Systems Laboratory in the Graduate School of Library and Information Science at the

University of Illinois at Urbana-Champaign, where he is working on his doctorate. During previous work as a graduate assistant in the Hypermedia Lab, he developed experimental hypermedia systems and was hired full time under the NSF Digital Library Initiative, which allowed him to extend his ideas about hypertext for use in thesaurus navigation and bibliographic retrieval.

DAVID LEVY was a member (until December 1999) of the Xerox Palo Alto Research Center (PARC) for fifteen years where his research focused on the nature of documents and on the tools and practices through which they are created and used. He is currently an independent consultant specializing in documents, digital libraries, and publishing. Dr. Levy is completing a book, "Scrolling Forward: Making Sense of Documents in a Digital Age," to be published by Arcade Publishing.

CATHERINE C. MARSHALL is a member of the research staff at the Xerox Palo Alto Research Center and an active participant in the International Hypertext, Digital Libraries, and WWW research communities. She has led a series of projects in the areas of spatial hypertext, collaborative hypernarrative, annotation, and metadata creation. Her work often crosses disciplinary boundaries; she collaborates with ethnographers, designers, and artists, as well as with her fellow computer scientists. Her home page can be found at http://www.csdl.tamu.edu/~marshall.

WILLIAM H. MISCHO is currently a member of the library faculty at the University of Illinois at Urbana-Champaign (UIUC). Prior to coming to the University of Illinois, Mr Mischo worked at OCLC and Iowa State University. His primary areas of research are in computer-user interaction and full-text databases. He served as a co-principal investigator for the Digital Library Initiative grant awarded to UIUC in 1994 and is presently co-principal investigator for a CNRI follow-on grant.

LAURA NEUMANN is a doctoral candidate in the Graduate School of Library and Information Science at the University of Illinois at Urbana-Champaign. Her main interests are the work practice and social issues surrounding the digitization of information, the use of digital libraries and other information systems, and the automation of work tasks. Her dissertation will focus on the work practice of humanities scholars and how and why digitized resources and information systems are or are not used.

DORBIN T. NG is a system scientist at the Robotics Institute of the Carnegie-Mellon University. He is currently finishing his doctoral degree at the University of Arizona. Mr. Ng has worked on knowledge networking and digital libraries related research since 1994. His work has appeared in *JASIS, IEEE Expert,* and *IEEE Computer.*

BRUCE R. SCHATZ is the Director of the Digital Library Research Program for the University Library at the University of Illinois at Urbana-Champaign.

MICHAEL TWIDALE is an Associate Professor, Graduate School of Library and Information Science at the University of Illinois at Urbana-Champaign. His interests include interactive learning environments, human computer interactions, usability design, collaborative learning, computer supported cooperative work, collaborative database browsing, digital libraries, and information visualization.

ROBERT WEDGEWORTH is former University Librarian and Professor of Library Administration at the University of Illinois at Urbana-Champaign. He has taught in graduate library education programs at the University of Chicago, Rutgers University, Columbia University, and at the University of Illinois. He is the founding editor of *World Encyclopedia of Library and Information Services* (3d ed., 1993) and has written numerous articles on library management, information policy, copyright and intellectual property, library technology, and international librarianship. Dr. Wedgeworth served as President of the International Federation of Library Associations and Institutions from 1991 to 1997.

INDEX

Prepared by Sandra Roe